TEXTS
OF
TERROR

OVERTURES TO BIBLICAL THEOLOGY

Editors

Literary-Feminist
Readings
of
Biblical
Narratives

TEXTS
OF
TERROR

PHYLLIS TRIBLE

FORTRESS PRESS   Philadelphia

Chapter 4 is an expanded version of "A Meditation in Mourning: The Sacrifice of the Daughter of Jephthah," previously published in the *Union Seminary Quarterly Review* 36 (1981):59–73. Used by permission.

Library of Congress Cataloging in Publication Data

Trible, Phyllis.
   Texts of terror.

   (Overtures to Biblical theology ; 13)
   Includes indexes.
   1. Women in the Bible. 2. Violence in the Bible.
3. Hidden God. I. Title. II. Series.
BS575.T74   1984   221.9′22   83–48906
ISBN 0–8006–1537–9

Printed in the U.S.A.   AF 1-1537

in memoriam

HELEN PRICE

MARY A. TULLY

Contents

Editor's Foreword

In her first book in this series, *God and the Rhetoric of Sexuality* (1978), Phyllis Trible offered a fresh way to listen to the text that permitted the text to have its own say, without excessive interpretive manipulation. By the time of this present book, Professor Trible has become established as one of the most effective practitioners of rhetorical criticism, and as perhaps the decisive voice in feminist exposition of biblical literature.

The studies offered in this book are the substance of her Beecher Lectures at Yale. That lecture series is intended to deal with the preaching enterprise in the church. Trible's perspective on exposition and proclamation is implicit and by example, without direct comment. She proposes to get the interpreter/expositor out of the way so that the unhindered text and the listening community can directly face each other.

What strikes me most about these expositions is the remarkable congruity between method and substance. That congruity has been a continuing agenda of scholarship, for we have become increasingly aware that conventional methods are essentially alien to the matter of the text and are something of an imposition on the text. The method utilized here makes very little, if any, imposition on the text. Trible presents a "state of the art" treatment of rhetorical criticism, learned from our common teacher James Muilenburg. It is hard to imagine the ground gained in the few years since he called for this methodological accent. Indeed, such a perspective was scarcely in purview in Old Testament studies when this series began. The remarkable fact about Trible's use of the method is that while she is fully conversant with literary theory, her presentation is free of every theoretical encumbrance.

But of course this book is not an exercise in method. It is the substance of the argument that makes the difference. The method, when utilized with fresh questions, lets us notice in the text the terror, violence, and pathos that more conventional methods have missed. Indeed this work makes clear how much the regnant methods, for all their claims of "objectivity," have indeed served the ideological ends of "the ruling class." What now surfaces is the history, consciousness, and cry of the victim, who in each case is shown to be a character of worth and dignity in the narrative. Heretofore, each has been regarded as simply an incidental prop for a drama about other matters. So Trible's "close reading" helps us notice. The presumed prop turns out to be a character of genuine interest, warranting our attention. And we are left to ask why our methods have reduced such characters, so that they have been lost to the story.

No doubt the feminist project of interpretation is much needed. The merit of Trible's feminist enterprise is that there is no special pleading, no stacking of the cards, no shrillness, no insistence. There is only the powerful, painful disclosure to us of what is there, so that the pain and shame have their undeniable say with us. Fittingly the method for such a reading is not pretentious or assertive. The outcome is not finally establishment of a method or pleading for a social ideology, but an insistence on the very character of the text. As our conventional methods have caused us to gloss over these victims, so this method causes us to notice the victim as an important presence. No doubt the method serves the cunning of the narrator who makes a statement that the censors of the establishment eagerly and readily fail to notice. The mark of this exposition is that it permits us to see what the text in fact speaks. And what the text in fact speaks is that hurt and terror are real and serious and cannot be excluded from the reading of any "true" story.

One other feature of Trible's work warrants attention. She is articulate, with a sure sense of what words do and how they sound and where they should be placed. The method of rhetorical criticism presumes that nothing is accidental but every word is intentional in its place. That is how it is with Trible's own words, as well as those of the text. Such sensitivity and care do honor to the preaching tradition of Beecher, which knows that words matter. And James Muilenburg would have endorsed this accomplishment as "felicitous."

WALTER BRUEGGEMANN

Abbreviations

ASV	American Standard Version
BR	*Biblical Research*
CBQ	*Catholic Biblical Quarterly*
Hermeneia	Hermeneia—A Critical and Historical Commentary on the Bible
HTR	*Harvard Theological Review*
ICC	International Critical Commentary
IDB	*Interpreter's Dictionary of the Bible*
IDBS	Supplementary Volume to *Interpreter's Dictionary of the Bible*
Int	*Interpretation*
Interpretation	Interpretation—A Bible Commentary for Teaching and Preaching
JB	Jerusalem Bible
JBL	*Journal of Biblical Literature*
JSOT	*Journal for the Study of the Old Testament*
JSOT Supp.	JSOT Supplement Series
KJV	King James Version
MT	Masoretic Text
NAB	New American Bible
NEB	New English Bible
NJV	New Jewish Version
OTL	Old Testament Library
RSV	Revised Standard Version
SBL	Society of Biblical Literature
VT	*Vetus Testamentum*
ZAW	*Zeitschrift für die alttestamentliche Wissenschaft*

Preface

In an earlier version these essays were the Lyman Beecher Lectures
delivered at Yale Divinity School, February 1982. Their title was
"Texts of Terror: Unpreached Stories of Faith." Selections from
them became parts of the 1982 Mackinnon Lectures at the Atlantic
School of Theology, Halifax, Nova Scotia; the 1983 Francis B.
Denio Lectures at Bangor Theological Seminary, Bangor, Maine;
and the 1983 Jackson Lectures at Perkins School of Theology, Dal-
las, Texas.

I have conceived this book as a companion to *God and the Rhetoric of Sexuality* (Philadelphia: Fortress Press, 1978). The two vol-
umes share a feminist perspective, a literary critical methodology,
and the subject matter of female and male in the Hebrew scriptures.
Yet the studies differ in emphasis and spirit. The first is a time to
laugh and dance; the second, a time to weep and mourn. Reversal
of the order of Qoheleth's rhythms (Eccl. 3:4) has proven crucial.
Without the joy of the first book, I should have found unbearable
the sorrow of the second. Ancient tales of terror speak all too fright-
eningly of the present.

If terror dominates the study, theory does not. Only a brief introduction stands between the reader and the stories, and no conclusion discusses what is narrated. Scholarly debate, methodological
defense, and theological disputation seldom appear in the text; such
burdens the footnotes bear. The resultant message is clear. Storytelling is sufficient unto itself.

Throughout I have employed different translations of the Bible.
Often I have quoted the Revised Standard Version, but more often
I have changed this text. Quotations thus altered are marked with
an asterisk after the abbreviation RSV (RSV*). Other published
translations are designated by their appropriate sigla. My own trans-

lations are left unmarked. I have designed them to convey Hebrew vocabulary and syntax, rather than felicitous English, and to use, where valid, nonsexist language.

A second type of markings also requires explanation. They pertain to the phenomenon of repetition as it is important for understanding the form, content, and meaning of the narratives. Repetition often signals the boundaries of literary units as well as the connection between units. It is an aid to memory and shows where emphasis lies. To indicate the presence of repetition in the relationships of words, phrases, clauses, or sentences, I have devised a series of indicators. Within a given section, a first group of repetitions is designated by <u>an unbroken line</u> under the language; a second group by <u>a broken line;</u> and a third by a set of dots. These indicators are arbitrarily chosen, but their use is purposeful and consistent.

In this pilgrimage of storytelling, many people have given me encouragement and expertise. I am particularly grateful to Ruthann Dwyer and Sarah Ryan for meticulous work and abiding interest. Each of them read the entire manuscript more than once, corrected mistakes, and suggested improvements. Special thanks also go to Toni Craven, Mary Ann Tolbert, and Julie Galas. Ms. Galas, secretary of the Biblical Field at Union Theological Seminary, typed innumerable drafts with patience, skill, and cheerfulness.

The two women to whom I dedicate the book manifested compassion for the sufferings of human beings. Helen Price was Professor of Ancient Languages at Meredith College, Raleigh, North Carolina, and Mary A. Tully, Associate Professor of Religious Education and Psychology at Union Theological Seminary, New York. In listing their academic titles, I render to Caesar. They themselves rendered to God, even the God of terror.

PHYLLIS TRIBLE

Texts of Terror

Introduction
On Telling Sad Stories

Stories are the style and substance of life. They fashion and fill existence. From primeval to eschatological vistas, from youthful dreams to seasoned experiences, from resounding disclosures to whispered intimacies, the narrative mode of speech prevails. Myth, parable, folk tale, epic, romance, novella, history, confession, biography—these and other genres proclaim the presence and power of the story.

If without stories we live not, stories live not without us. Alone a text is mute and ineffectual.[1] In the speaking and the hearing new things appear in the land. The word goes forth from the mouth; even the tongue of the stammerer speaks readily and distinctly. The ears of those who hear hearken; even the ears of the deaf unstop. Thus the word does not return empty but accomplishes that which it purposes.[2] Storytelling is a trinitarian act that unites writer, text, and reader in a collage of understanding.[3] Though distinguishable and unequal, the three participants are inseparable and interdependent. Truly, "in the tale, in the telling, we are all one blood."[4]

In this book my task is to tell sad stories as I hear them. Indeed, they are tales of terror with women as victims. Belonging to the sacred scriptures of synagogue and church, these narratives yield four portraits of suffering in ancient Israel: Hagar, the slave used, abused, and rejected; Tamar, the princess raped and discarded; an unnamed woman, the concubine raped, murdered, and dismembered; and the daughter of Jephthah, a virgin slain and sacrificed.

Choice and chance inspire my telling these particular tales: hearing a black woman describe herself as a daughter of Hagar outside the covenant; seeing an abused woman on the streets of New York

1

with a sign, "My name is Tamar"; reading news reports of the dismembered body of a woman found in a trash can; attending worship services in memory of nameless women; and wrestling with the silence, absence, and opposition of God. All these experiences and others have led me to a land of terror from whose bourn no traveler returns unscarred. The journey is solitary and intense. In joining this venture, the reader assumes its risks.

PITFALLS AND GUIDES

Yet the reader need not enter unawares. Having already made the journey, the writer knows the terrain. From the start, certain theological positions constitute pitfalls. They center in Christian chauvinism. First, to account for these stories as relics of a distant, primitive, and inferior past is invalid. Resoundingly, the evidence of history refutes all claims to the superiority of a Christian era.[5] Second, to contrast an Old Testament God of wrath with a New Testament God of love is fallacious. The God of Israel is the God of Jesus, and in both testaments resides tension between divine wrath and divine love. Third, to subordinate the suffering of the four women to the suffering of the cross is spurious. Their passion has its own integrity; no comparisons diminish the terror they knew. Fourth, to seek the redemption of these stories in the resurrection is perverse. Sad stories do not have happy endings.

Offsetting these pitfalls are guides for telling and hearing the tales. To perceive the Bible as a mirror is one such sign. If art imitates life, scripture likewise reflects it in both holiness and horror. Reflections themselves neither mandate nor manufacture change; yet by enabling insight, they may inspire repentance. In other words, sad stories may yield new beginnings.

To use scripture in interpreting scripture is a second guide for the journey.[6] Pondering an individual narrative evokes associations with other texts; studying other texts illuminates a single story. This kind of dialectic informs my telling sad tales. Among the many scriptural allusions I employ throughout the essays, three sets of passages constitute leitmotifs: the suffering servant songs of Second Isaiah, the passion narratives of the Gospels, and the eucharistic sections of the Pauline Epistles. These familiar passages receive, however, unfamiliar applications.[7] Women, not men, are suffering servants and Christ figures. Their stories govern the use of the leitmotifs. Scripture thus interpreting scripture undercuts triumphalism and raises disturbing questions for faith.

PROVISIONS FOR THE JOURNEY

In addition to the guides for telling and hearing these texts, certain provisions sustain the journey. They are few but ample: a perspective, a methodology, and a story. Jacob's wrestling at the Jabbok is the story; literary criticism, the methodology; and feminism, the perspective.

As a critique of culture and faith in light of misogyny, feminism is a prophetic movement, examining the status quo, pronouncing judgment, and calling for repentance. This hermeneutic engages scripture in various ways.[8] One approach documents the case against women. It cites and evaluates long neglected data that show the inferiority, subordination, and abuse of the female in ancient Israel and the early church. By contrast, a second approach discerns within the Bible critiques of patriarchy. It upholds forgotten texts and reinterprets familiar ones to shape a remnant theology that challenges the sexism of scripture.[9] Yet a third approach incorporates the other two. It recounts tales of terror *in memoriam* to offer sympathetic readings of abused women. If the first perspective documents misogyny historically and sociologically, this one appropriates the data poetically and theologically. At the same time, it continues to search for the remnant in unlikely places. Such an approach characterizes these essays. It interprets stories of outrage on behalf of their female victims in order to recover a neglected history, to remember a past that the present embodies, and to pray that these terrors shall not come to pass again. In telling sad stories, a feminist hermeneutic seeks to redeem the time.

Joining this perspective is the methodology of literary criticism.[10] As practiced here, it involves an intrinsic reading of the text in its final form.[11] The phrase "intrinsic reading" means wholly upon the text rather than wholly within the text.[12] To elicit understanding, analysis brings conventions to literature. These learned procedures, tools, and controls vary from critic to critic and from age to age.[13] For this study, accent is upon the inseparability of form, content, and meaning; the rhetorical formation of sentences, episodes, and scenes as well as overall design and plot structure;[14] and the portrayal of characters, most especially the violated women.

Each essay stands on its own; conversely, each belongs to the other three as variations upon the theme of terror. Independence and interdependence thus order the chapters. On the one hand, no particular arrangement is mandatory. On the other hand, dramatic effect has shaped the sequence. From rejection to rape to dismemberment to sacrifice, literary judgments supersede historical claims.

If literary criticism is the methodology and feminism the perspective, Jacob's wrestling at the Jabbok provides the story for our journey (Gen. 32:22–32).[15] On his way home after years of sojourn, Jacob spends a night alone in combat against an inscrutable opponent.[16] The story suggests that this "man" (*'îš*) is deity, and yet a precise identity remains uncertain.[17] Darkness by the river Jabbok conceals meaning while revealing the perplexity and terror of the event.

The fight is close to an even match. As Jacob prevails, the man puts out of joint the hollow of Jacob's thigh. Their physical struggle yields to a verbal contest, with Jacob refusing to let the man go unless he blesses him. The night visitor deflects this demand by eliciting a confession of the name Jacob as trickster, cheater, or supplanter.[18] To reorient the identity of the patriarch, he changes that name to Israel ("God rules"). But again, Jacob wants to trick the assailant. "Tell me, I pray, your name," he asks. Although the request demonstrates a continuing desire for power, it is defeated by an all-knowing question, "Why is it that you ask my name?" Only then does the powerful opponent bless the mighty striver. What Jacob wants, he does not get on his own terms. The outcome acknowledges both the crippling victory and the magnificent defeat of that night.[19] Jacob's life is preserved, but he limps as he leaves the Jabbok.

As a paradigm for encountering terror, this story offers sustenance for the present journey. To tell and hear tales of terror is to wrestle demons in the night, without a compassionate God to save us. In combat we wonder about the names of the demons. Our own names, however, we all too frightfully recognize. The fight itself is solitary and intense. We struggle mightily, only to be wounded. But yet we hold on, seeking a blessing: the healing of wounds and the restoration of health. If the blessing comes—and we dare not claim assurance—it does not come on our terms. Indeed, as we leave the land of terror, we limp.

With pitfalls to shun, guides to follow, and provisions to use, the trinitarian act of storytelling engages four texts of terror.

NOTES

1. See Paul Ricoeur, *Interpretation Theory* (Fort Worth: Texas Christian University Press, 1976), p. 75.

2. For the scriptural allusions in the preceding sentences, see Jer. 31:22b; Isa. 32:3–4; 35:5; 55:10–11.

3. On the teller and the tale, see Robert Scholes and Robert Kellogg, *The Nature of Narrative* (New York and London: Oxford University Press, 1966); Mary McCarthy, "Novel, Tale, Romance," *The New York Review of Books*, 12 May 1983, pp. 49–56; on the reader, see Wolfgang Iser, *The Act of Reading* (Baltimore: Johns Hopkins University Press, 1980). Though I concentrate on these three participants, other critics may also take into account, e.g., the implied author and the implied reader. See Wayne C. Booth, *The Rhetoric of Fiction* (Chicago: University of Chicago Press, 1961); Wolfgang Iser, *The Implied Reader* (Baltimore: Johns Hopkins University Press, 1978); Susan R. Suleiman and Inge Crossman, eds., *The Reader in the Text* (Princeton, N.J.: Princeton University Press, 1980). For helpful discussions of all these and related issues, see Shlomith Rimmon-Kenan, *Narrative Fiction: Contemporary Poetics* (London: Methuen & Co., 1983) and Terry Eagleton, *Literary Theory: An Introduction* (Minneapolis: University of Minnesota Press, 1983).

4. Ursula K. LeGuin, "It Was a Dark and Stormy Night; or, Why Are We Huddling about the Campfire?" in *On Narrative*, ed. W. J. T. Mitchell (Chicago: University of Chicago Press, 1981), p. 195. LeGuin continues, "Take the tale in your teeth, then, and bite till the blood runs, hoping it's not poison; and we will all come to the end together, and even to the beginning: living, as we do, in the middle."

5. Examples are superfluous, though in our own time one thinks of the nuclear attacks on Hiroshima and Nagasaki; Nazi death camps; the slaughter in Vietnam; atrocities in El Salvador, including the murders of four religious women; and the massacre of the Palestinians in Beirut. For individual stories of terror, one need only read the newspaper, talk to friends and strangers, or look within.

6. For discussions and examples of this principle in all its diversity, see, *inter alia*, G. W. H. Lampe and K. J. Woolcombe, *Essays on Typology* (Naperville, Ill.: Alec R. Allenson, 1957); Brevard S. Childs, *Biblical Theology in Crisis* (Philadelphia: Westminster Press, 1960), pp. 139–219; James D. Smart, *The Interpretation of Scripture* (Philadelphia: Westminster Press, 1961); Beryl Smalley, *The Study of the Bible in the Middle Ages* (Notre Dame, Ind.: University of Notre Dame Press, 1978); Claus Westermann,

ed., *Essays on Old Testament Hermeneutics* (Atlanta: John Knox Press, 1979); Robert M. Grant with David Tracy, *A Short History of the Interpretation of the Bible*, 2d ed. rev. and enl. (Philadelphia: Fortress Press, 1984). Though my concern is focused on biblical passages, extrabiblical literature, ancient and modern, can also be used to illuminate scripture. See, e.g., David Robertson, *The Old Testament and the Literary Critic* (Philadelphia: Fortress Press, 1977).

7. Whether implicitly or explicitly, application includes both similarities and differences among texts. What is stressed depends upon the needs of the occasion, the disposition of the interpreter, and the substance of the texts. The process involves a controlled subjectivity that is avowedly selective.

8. See Phyllis Trible, "Feminist Hermeneutics and Biblical Studies," *The Christian Century* (3–10 February 1982): 116–18; Phyllis Bird, "Images of Women in the Old Testament," in *Religion and Sexism*, ed. Rosemary Radford Ruether (New York: Simon & Schuster, 1974), pp. 41–88; Carol Meyers, "The Roots of Restriction: Women in Early Israel," *Biblical Archeologist* 41 (1978): 91–103; Katharine Doob Sakenfeld, "Old Testament Perspectives: Methodological Issues," *JSOT* 22 (1982): 13–20; Carol Meyers, "Procreation, Production, and Protection," *JAAR* 51 (1983).

9. Phyllis Trible, *God and the Rhetoric of Sexuality* (Philadelphia: Fortress Press, 1978), exemplifies this approach.

10. Though literary study of the Bible is currently enjoying a new press, it has a long, rich, and well-established history. Moreover, the Bible itself has been a major paradigm in the literary history of the West. See James L. Kugel, *The Idea of Biblical Poetry: Parallelism and Its History* (New Haven, Conn.: Yale University Press, 1981), especially chapter six and the references cited therein.

11. Such considerations as historical background, sociological setting, compositional history, authorial intention, and linguistic and archaeological data are essential in the total exegetical enterprise, but in literary analysis they are supporting rather than primary concerns. The emphasis here is artful composition. See Chaim Potok, "The Bible's Inspired Art," *The New York Times Magazine*, 3 October 1982, pp. 58–68; David J. A. Clines, "Methods in Old Testament Study," in *Beginning Old Testament Study*, ed. John Rogerson (Philadelphia: Westminster Press, 1982), pp. 33–38.

12. The point is that even an intrinsic reading depends upon matters extrinsic to the text, e.g., theories of language and literature as well as a vocabulary other than the verbatim text.

13. See James L. Kugel, "On the Bible and Literary Criticism," *Prooftexts* (1981): 217–36; also Adele Berlin and James L. Kugel, "On the Bible as Literature," *Prooftexts* (1982): 323–32.

14. See James Muilenburg, "Form Criticism and Beyond," *JBL* 88 (1969): 1–18. For recent literary studies of biblical narratives, see Robert Alter, *The Art of Biblical Narrative* (New York: Basic Books, 1981); Kenneth R. R. Gros Louis, ed., *Literary Interpretations of Biblical Narratives*, vol. 2 (Nashville: Abingdon Press, 1982); David J. A. Clines, David M. Gunn, and Alan J. Houser, eds., *Art and Meaning: Rhetoric in Biblical Literature*, JSOT Supp. 19 (Sheffield: JSOT Press, 1982).

15. See Walter Brueggemann, *Genesis*, Interpretation (Atlanta: John Knox Press, 1982), pp. 266–74; Walter Wink, "On Wrestling with God," *Religion in Life* 47 (1978): 136–47.

16. Note that the narrative is exclusively male. Only after Jacob has sent his wives, his maids, and his children across the stream does "a man" wrestle with him. See Linda Clark, "A Sermon: Wrestling with Jacob's Angel," *Image-breaking/Image-building*, ed. Linda Clark, Marian Ronan, and Eleanor Walker (New York: Pilgrim Press, 1981), pp. 98–104.

17. Hosea 12:3–4 describes the divine visitor as an angel *(maľāk).*

18. Brueggemann, *Genesis*, p. 268; Gerhard von Rad, *Genesis*, OTL (Philadelphia: Westminster Press, 1961), p. 321.

19. Cf. Brueggemann, *Genesis*, p. 270, and Frederick Buechner, *The Magnificient Defeat* (New York: Seabury Press, 1966), pp. 10–26.

HAGAR

Egyptian Slave Woman

She was wounded for
our transgressions;
she was bruised for
our iniquities.

CHAPTER 1

Hagar
The Desolation of Rejection

Genesis 16:1–16; 21: 9–21

Though Abraham prevails in scripture as the symbol of faith, his story pivots on two women, Sarah and Hagar, who shape and challenge faith. Their own stories diverge to give Sarah the better portion. Wife of a wealthy herdsman (Gen. 13:2), she holds privilege and power within the confines of patriarchal structures.[1] To be sure, on two occasions Abraham betrays her, passing her off as his sister to protect himself (12:10–20; 20:1–19),[2] but each time God comes to her rescue. Without effort, this woman along with her husband enjoys divine favor. Yet her exaltation poses major tension in Abram's story because "Sarai is barren; she has no child" (11:30, RSV*).[3] Moreover, "it has ceased to be with Sarah after the manner of women" (18:11, RSV*; cf. 17:17). Her situation would seem to thwart the divine promise of an heir for Abram.[4] Hence, Sarai plans to secure a child through her maid Hagar, who becomes the other woman in Abram's life.

As one of the first females in scripture to experience use, abuse, and rejection, Hagar the Egyptian slave claims our attention. Knowledge of her has survived in bits and pieces only, from the oppressor's perspective at that, and so our task is precarious: to tell Hagar's story from the fragments that remain.

These fragments come from separate scenes in the Abrahamic saga.[5] The first (16:1–16) precedes by several chapters and the second (21:9–21) just follows the birth of the child God eventually gives to Sarah herself.[6] Similar structures and subjects order the scenes. In both, narrative introductions and conclusions surround two episodes. The opening episodes, located in Canaan, highlight Sarah as

9

she deals with Hagar and Abraham; the closing ones, located in the wilderness, feature Hagar encountering the deity. Besides providing continuity, these structural and content parallels between the scenes highlight their differences. For Hagar, the plot of the first story is circular, moving from bondage to flight to bondage, while the action of the second is linear, proceeding from bondage to expulsion to homelessness.[7]

A CIRCLE OF BONDAGE

Scene One: Genesis 16:1–16

A. *Introduction, 16:1.* The opening sentence of scene one emphasizes Sarai. Reversing the usual Hebrew word order, it places before the verb her name as subject. "Now Sarai, wife of Abram, did not bear a child to him" (16:1). The statement of the problem leads in the second half of the sentence to an answer. "But to her [was] an Egyptian maid whose name was Hagar."[8] Beginning with Sarai and ending with Hagar, the narrated introduction opposes two women around the man Abram. Sarai the Hebrew is married, rich, and free; she is also old and barren. Hagar the Egyptian is single, poor, and bonded;[9] she is also young and fertile. Power belongs to Sarai, the subject of action; powerlessness marks Hagar, the object.

B. *Episode One, 16:2–6.* From the introduction the story moves to its first episode. At the beginning, Sarai speaks in the imperative mood.[10] Dialogic order and verb construction match content to present this woman as the commanding figure. While confirming the problem and solution that the storyteller has reported, she makes subtle changes:

> And Sarai said to Abram,
>   "Because Yahweh has prevented me
>   from bearing children,
>   go to my maid.
>   Perhaps I shall be built up from her."
>   (16:2a)

Unlike the narrator, Sarai speaks of building up herself through Hagar rather than of bearing a child to Abram (cf. 16:1, 15). In a man's world, the woman's voice sounds a different emphasis.[11] Further, unlike the narrator, she attributes her barren plight to Yahweh and thus seeks to counter divine action with human initiative. What the deity has prevented, Sarai can accomplish through the maid whose name she never utters and to whom she never speaks.[12] For Sarai, Hagar is an instrument, not a person. The maid enhances the mistress.

Sarai's words effect obedience. Abram makes no attempt to halt the plan; instead, he yields so passively that the storyteller must answer for him. "And Abram heard [obeyed] the voice of Sarai" (16:2b). Continuing to underline *his* acquiescence, the narrated discourse reports *her* action:*

> Sarai, wife of Abram, took Hagar the Egyptian, her maid,
>   after Abram had dwelt ten years in the land of Canaan,
> and gave her to Abram her husband, to him for a wife.
>   (16:3)

Again in the structure of a sentence, two females encircle Abram (cf. 16:1). And they are unequally matched. As subject of the verbs *take* and *give*, Sarai exercises power over Hagar, the object. Though her actions relate the two women, the absence of dialogue maintains distance between them. Repeated use of the relational language wife, maid, husband, and wife accents the growing opposition. In making Hagar Abram's wife, not his concubine,[13] Sarai has diminished her own status in relationship to this servant. But she still retains full control over Abram. As he first obeyed her voice in a narrated sentence of few words, so now he fulfills her command, "Go (bō'), then, into ('el) my maid" (16:2). "And he went (bō') into ('el) Hagar" (16:4a, RSV).[14] No mighty patriarch is Abram, but rather the silent, acquiescent, and minor figure in a drama between two women.

Sarai has spoken; Abram has agreed. Sarai has acted; Abram has obeyed. Next the plot shifts to Hagar, the one through whom Sarai wishes to be built up. Making the maid subject, not object, the narrator reports, "She conceived" (16:4b). Although this result is what Sarai wants, it prompts an insight on Hagar's part that her mistress

* For an explanation of the underlinings in this and subsequent units, see the Preface, p. xiv.

has not anticipated. "When she [Hagar] saw that she had conceived, her mistress was slight in her eyes" (16:4c). Hagar is other than a tool; for that difference Sarai has failed to allow.

The Hebrew expression "her mistress was slight (or trifling) in her eyes" inspires various interpretations. Many translators alter the syntax to make Hagar the subject of the verb. They also attribute to the verb (*qll*) the legitimate, though not necessary, meaning of contempt or disdain. Accordingly, one reads, "When she knew she was with child, she despised her mistress" (NEB); or "when she saw that she had conceived, she looked with contempt on her mistress" (RSV).[15] Yet the verb with its correct subject also offers the less harsh reading that is present in the translation, "Her mistress was lowered in her esteem" (NJV).

Although strife between barren and fertile wives is a typical motif in scripture,[16] in this study the typical yields to the particular. Seeing, that is, perceiving her conception of a child, Hagar acquires a new vision of Sarai. Hierarchical blinders disappear. The exalted mistress decreases while the lowly maid increases. Not hatred but a reordering of the relationship is the point. Unwittingly, Sarai has contributed to Hagar's insight. By giving Hagar to Abram for a wife, Sarai hoped to be built up. In fact, however, she has enhanced the status of the servant to become herself correspondingly lowered in the eyes of Hagar.

This unexpected twist provides an occasion for mutuality and equality between two females, but it is not to be. If Hagar has experienced new vision, Sarai remains within the old structures.[17] Still in charge, she speaks to Abram, faulting him for the outcome of her plan and appealing to Yahweh for judgment. While she uses the same vocabulary as the narrator to describe Hagar's response, the words on her lips have a pejorative meaning:[18]

> And Sarai said to Abram,
> "May the wrong done to me be upon you!
>
> I (*'ānōkî*) gave my maid to your embrace
> but when she saw that she had conceived,
> then I was slight in her eyes.
>
> May Yahweh judge between you and me!"
> (16:5, RSV*)

The mistress wants returned the superior status that she unintentionally relinquished in using Hagar. Further, she demands that her husband rectify the wrong because he holds authority over Hagar too. But Abram, speaking for the first time in this scene, chooses not to exercise power and thus remains passive:[19]

> But Abram said to Sarai,
> "Since your maid is in your hand,
> do to her the good in your eyes."
> (16:6a)

The idiom, "the good in your eyes," plays upon the reference to Hagar's eyes: "Her mistress was slight in her eyes." The vision of the mistress opposes the insight of the maid. What is good for the one is suffering for the other.

If Sarai's opening speech to Abram ordered the use of Hagar (16:2), her words to him now, with his reply, lead to the abuse of the maid. Succinctly, the narrator declares, "And Sarai afflicted her" (16:6b). Once again the two women meet unequally as subject and object, vanquisher and victim, and this time Hagar has lost her name (cf. 16:3). Moreover, the absence of dialogue continues to separate the females. Inequality, opposition, and distance breed violence. "Sarai afflicted her." The verb *afflict* (*'nh*) is a strong one, connoting harsh treatment. It characterizes, for example, the sufferings of the entire Hebrew population in Egypt, the land of their bondage.[20] Ironically, here it depicts the torture of a lone Egyptian woman in Canaan, the land of her bondage to the Hebrews. Sarai afflicted Hagar.

In conceiving a child for her mistress, Hagar has seen a new reality that challenges the power structure. Her vision leads not to a softening but to an intensification of the system. In the hand of Sarai, with the consent of Abram, Hagar becomes the suffering servant, the precursor of Israel's plight under Pharaoh. Yet no deity comes to deliver her from bondage and oppression; nor does she beseech one. Instead, this tortured female claims her own exodus. "Sarai afflicted her, and so she fled (*brh*) from her"—even as Israel will later flee (*brh*) from Pharaoh (Exod. 14:5a). Thus, episode one closes with Hagar taking command of her own life under the threat of Sarai.

de Two, 16:7–14. The opening of episode two plays upon
~~ᴜᴜᴜ~~ng:

And Sarai afflicted her.
So she fled from her.

But the messenger of the Lord found her.
(16:6b–7a)

In the first and third sentences, Hagar is the direct object of verbs
with different subjects. While the afflicting of her by Sarai is hostile
treatment, the finding of her by the deity holds uncertain meaning.
The divine action may either counter or confirm Sarai's action. If
the finding counters the afflicting, then the flight of Hagar in the
middle of the sequence signals a new direction that the diety enhances, encourages, and, in fact, empowers. But if the finding confirms the afflicting, then the flight of Hagar is a futile activity that
the deity circumscribes, controls, and, in fact, cancels. The juxtaposition of the three sentences poses ambiguity in the development
of the narrative. Resolution awaits further action by the messenger
of the Lord.

Before continuing with the divine action, the storyteller provides
a brief note about Hagar's location. Like Israel in years to come,
this runaway pregnant maid has fled from the house of bondage to
the wilderness. For her it is a hospitable place, symbolized by a
spring on the way to Shur, a region at the Egyptian border.[21] There,
with water to nourish life, Hagar is almost home. How different are
her circumstances from Israel's exodus! When "Moses led Israel
onward from the Red Sea, and they went into the wilderness of Shur,
they went three days in the wilderness and found no water" (Exod.
15:22, RSV). Indeed, Moses had to ask the Lord for water. But
Hagar does not cry out to any god, most especially not to Yahweh
whose action in closing Sarai's womb has brought affliction to the
maidservant. Nevertheless, like Moses, Hagar encounters deity
after she has fled from her oppressor (cf. Exod. 2:15b–16; 3:1–2).[22]
The messenger of Yahweh finds her by the spring of water in the
wilderness. This Egyptian maid is the first person in scripture whom
such a messenger visits.[23]

Speech alone reveals the divine presence. "Hagar, maid of Sarai, from where have you come and where are you going?" (16:8a, RSV). For the first time a character speaks to Hagar and uses her name. The deity acknowledges what Sarai and Abram have not: the personhood of this woman. Yet the appositive, "maid of Sarai," tempers the recognition, for Hagar remains a servant in the vocabulary of the divine. Rather than freeing her from a human bond of servitude, "the messenger of the Lord" (16:7) addresses "the maid of Sarai" (16:8). These relational identifications pose a striking contrast even as they harbor a parallel meaning. To be "of Sarai" is to be "of the Lord."

"From where have you come and where are you going?" The questions embody origin and destiny. In answering, Hagar speaks for the first time. Exodus from oppression liberates her voice, though full personhood continues to elude her. Subtly, the narrator suggests this limitation by omitting her name throughout the entire episode, most particularly in the introductions to her speeches.[24] Only feminine verb forms or pronouns identify Hagar. She herself acknowledges this incompleteness of personhood in replying to the divine question, "From where have you come?" While she answers in the same syntactical order that the question was posed, she transforms the content of both the prepositional phrase and the verb. "And she said, 'From the face of Sarai, my mistress, I (*'ānōkî*) am fleeing'" (16:8b). "From where have you come?" From a place she has not come; rather, from a person she is fleeing. Matching the messenger's designation, "maid of Sarai," the phrase, "Sarai my mistress," indicates the continuing power of the social structure. Exodus from oppression has not secured freedom for Hagar. She continues, however, to resist. "I (*'ānōkî*)," she says emphatically, "am fleeing." This *I* stands over against the *I* (*'ānōkî*) of Sarai (16:5). Powerlessness defies power.

"Where are you going?" is the second question. Hagar seems not to answer. Or is departure her destiny? After all, the wilderness signifies escape from oppression, nourishment of life, and revelation of the divine. But if for her departure is destiny, for the messenger of the Lord a different answer prevails. The appositives, "maid of Sarai," and "Sarai my mistress," indicate that the past invades the present to shape the future. Hence, wilderness is not destination but point of return. "The messenger of the Lord" has found "the maid of Sarai" in order to tell her where she is going. And the divine command merges origin and destiny: "Return to your mistress, and suffer affliction under her hand" (16:9). Truly, to be "of Sarai" is to be "of the Lord."

Double imperatives underscore the severity. By itself the order "Return to your mistress" might mean reversion to the beginning when servitude existed apart from harsh treatment. But the second command negates such an interpretation: "Suffer affliction under her hand." The verb ('nh) is the same word used for Sarai's earlier abuse of Hagar (16:6b). Further, the phrase, *under her hand*, echoes Abram's reply to Sarai, "Look, your maid is *in your hand*; do to her the good in your eyes" (16:6a).

Without doubt, these two imperatives, return and submit to suffering, bring a divine word of terror to an abused, yet courageous, woman. They also strike at the heart of Exodus faith. Inexplicably, the God who later, seeing (r'h) the suffering ('ŏnî) of a slave people, comes down to deliver them *out of the hand* of the Egyptians (Exod. 3:7-8) here identifies with the oppressor and orders a servant to return not only to bondage but also to affliction.[25] Thus, the ambiguity present at the beginning of this episode finds its resolution in the approval of affliction. "Sarai afflicted her" (16:6b) and "the messenger of the Lord found her" (16:7a) are parallel in form and meaning. Surrounded by these sentences, Hagar's flight is futile.

To be sure, two promises attend the divine command to return and suffer affliction, but each is fraught with ambivalence.[26] The first assures Hagar of innumerable descendants. "I will so greatly multiply your descendants that they cannot be numbered for multitude" (16:10, RSV). While all the patriarchs of Israel hear such words,[27] Hagar is the only woman ever to receive them. And yet this promise to her lacks the covenant context that is so crucial to the founding fathers.

From this assurance of innumerable descendants the focus narrows, in the second promise, to the birth announcement of a child.[28] Although Hagar knows that she is pregnant, the divine messenger sanctions what has come through human machinations. The annunciation has three basic elements: the prediction of the birth of a male child, the naming of the child, and the future life of the child.[29]

Truly you are pregnant
and will bear a son.

You will call his name Ishmael,
for Yahweh has paid heed to your affliction.

He will be a wild ass of a man,
his hand against everyone and everyone's
hand against him.
And against the face of all his brothers
he will dwell.

(16:11–12, RSV*)

As the first to receive an annunciation, Hagar the Egyptian is the prototype of special mothers in Israel.[30] For her the unborn child signifies not just comfort but also suffering. The name Ishmael ("God hears") affirms the two meanings.[31] While Hagar has never cried out to God, the deity pays heed to her past affliction (*'nh*; 16:6) by assuring her a future through the son.[32] The promise would seem to negate Sarai's plan to be built up through Hagar.[33] Thus hope prevails. On the other hand, the deity has already paid heed to Hagar's affliction by ordering her to submit further (*'nh*; 16:9) to Sarai in the present. Suffering undercuts hope. A sword pierces Hagar's own soul. The divine promise of Ishmael means life at the boundary of consolation and desolation.

The ending of this birth announcement turns from mother to son. Concern for the male deflects interest from the female. Ishmael is to be a wanderer and loner, in strife even with his own people. Two words in the description, however, reflect Hagar's story: *hand* and *face*. "His *hand* [will be] against everyone and everyone's *hand* against him" (16:12b). Such language recalls Abram's words to Sarai, "Look now, your maid is in your *hand*" (16:6), as well as Yahweh's orders to Hagar, "Return to your mistress and suffer affliction under her *hand*" (16:9). If Hagar lives under the hand of Sarai, the hand of Ishmael will engage in ceaseless strife against such power. Indeed, "against the *face* of all his brothers he will dwell" (16:12c). The word *face* builds upon his mother's action when she said, "From the *face* of Sarai my mistress I am fleeing" (16:8). In Ishmael, Hagar's story continues.

Responding to these ambivalent promises from the heavenly messenger, Hagar "calls the name of Yahweh who has spoken to her"

(16:13a). The expression is striking because it connotes naming rather than invocation. In other words, Hagar does not call *upon* the name of the deity (*qr' bšm yhwh*; cf. Gen. 12:8; 13:4). Instead, she calls the name (*qr' šm-yhwh*), a power attributed to no one else in all the Bible. "She calls the name of Yahweh who has spoken to her, 'You are a God of seeing'" (16:13b).[34] The maid who, after seeing (*r'h*) her conception of a child, had a new vision of her mistress Sarai (16:4), now, after receiving a divine announcement of the forthcoming birth, sees (*r'h*) God with new vision.[35] Hagar is a theologian. Her naming unites the divine and human encounter: the God who sees and the God who is seen.[36]

To this name she attaches an explanation. It yields confusion because the Hebrew is obscure. "For she said, 'Have I even here seen (*r'h*) after the one who sees (*r'h*) me?'" (16:13c).[37] Perhaps Hagar is questioning her own understanding of the revelation she has just received. The God who sees her remains unclear to her. Following this elusive comment, the narrator adds an aetiological note identifying her location as "the well of the living one who sees (*r'h*) me" (16:14a). But the connection between her words and her locale is also nebulous.[38] In the end, then, the meaning of Hagar's question remains uncertain. We know only that the maid who names the deity "God of seeing" must return to the suffering that Yahweh imposes upon her, specifically to the mistress who is slight in her eyes. A circle of bondage encloses Hagar.

D. *Conclusion, 16:15–16.* Of her return and affliction under Sarai the storyteller says nothing. Instead, scene one concludes with a formulaic report of the birth of Ishmael that exalts Abram:[39]

> And Hagar bore to Abram a son,
>> and Abram called the name of his son,
>>> whom Hagar bore, Ishmael.
> Now Abram was eighty-six years old
>> when Hagar bore Ishmael to Abram.

                                                    (16:15–16, RSV*)

The very first word of the story was Sarai (16:1); the last is Abram. The introduction sounded the negative note, "did not bear a child to him." The conclusion responds with the positive word, "bore

Ishmael to Abram." Moving the story from a sad beginning to a happy ending is Hagar. Yet throughout, her own story runs counter to this movement.

Not surprisingly, the narrated ending continues to undermine Hagar. First, though it restores her name, it silences her voice. Second, it stresses not her motherhood but the fatherhood of Abram,[40] whom the messenger of Yahweh never mentioned. Third, in reporting that Abram named the son Ishmael, it strips Hagar of the power that God gave her. Moreover, the ending undercuts Sarai. The one who spoke of building up herself, not Abram, through Hagar's child receives no mention at all. Neither Hagar nor Sarai but Abram has a son whom he names Ishmael. Patriarchy is well in control. This conclusion to a scene otherwise focused on women resumes Abram's story.

THE WAY OF TRANSITION

Genesis 17:1—21:8. The resumption of Abram's story brings changes to all the characters. No longer Abram and Sarai, the patriarch and his wife become Abraham and Sarah (17:5, 15). Hagar disappears, but her story remains. Ishmael becomes the object of divine rejection precisely because Hagar, not Sarah, is his mother (17:15-21). Thus Abraham's story continues to pivot on these two women, and again Sarah receives the better portion: the divine promise of her very own son (18:1-15).[41] Yet the matriarch laughs to herself about the possibility of bearing a child in her old age (18:12). Unlike Hagar, Sarah is never the recipient of a birth announcement. In fact, Yahweh speaks to her just once, and then with a curt reprimand for disbelieving laughter (18:15).

Promise and delay, doubt and deception move to the advent of Isaac whom Sarah bears to Abraham through the grace of God (21:1-8).[42] Her response to this miraculous birth suggests that she is built up, not in herself, however, but in giving Abraham a son:

Who would have said to Abraham,
    "Children Sarah will nurse"?
Yet (*kî*) I have borne him a son
    in his old age.[43]
(21:7, RSV*)

What the culture expects of Sarah, what she has tried to accomplish through her maid, God has at last given her. Yet, rather than alleviating her trouble with Hagar, the presence of Isaac intensifies it. Hence, additional fragments of Hagar's story emerge in a second scene.

A LINE TO EXILE

Scene Two: Genesis 21:9–21

Though similar in design to scene one, scene two has a more complicated plot. Ishmael and Isaac enlarge the cast of characters to bring other changes. In contrast to its parallel (16:2–6), the first episode (21:9–14abc) portrays Sarah speaking less while accomplishing more, Abraham not speaking but resisting, God intervening directly, and Hagar suffering increasingly.

A. *Introduction and Episode One, 21:9–14abc.* The narrator introduces the story by hinting at further tension between the two women. Sarah provokes it.

> Now Sarah saw the son of Hagar the Egyptian,
>   whom she had borne to Abraham, playing.[44]
>   (21:9, RSV*)

The description "the son of Hagar the Egyptian" highlights mother, not child. The phrase "whom she had borne to Abraham" recalls Sarai's role in making Hagar Abram's wife. And the verb *see (r'h)*, which describes Sarah's activity, earlier reported Hagar's response to pregnancy: "When she saw *(r'h)* that she had conceived, her mistress was slight in her eyes" (16:4c). Now Sarah sees the fruit of this conception. Thus, enmity persists between the Hebrew mistress and her Egyptian maid.

What the narrator suggests, Sarah's words confirm, indeed exacerbate. Constructing opposition on inequality, she commands Abraham:

> Cast out *(grš)* this slave woman and her son,
>   for the son of this slave woman will not inherit
>   with my son, with Isaac.
>   (21:10, RSV*)

The presence of Ishmael in Canaan plagues the future of Isaac, whose inheritance is threatened.[45] In her move to eliminate the danger, Sarah debases Hagar and Ishmael while exalting herself and Isaac. The phrase "her son," without the name Ishmael,[46] counters "my son . . . Isaac." The description "this slave woman," rather than "my maid" (cf. 16:2), increases distance between Hagar and Sarah.[47] Not only is the possessive adjective *my* missing, but also a change in nouns connotes a change in status. From being a maid (*šiphâ*) to Sarai in scene one, Hagar has become a slave (*'āmâ*), serving the master of the house as his second wife.[48] By contrast, Sarah, the first wife, enjoys power greater than ever because she has born a son. As the life of the mistress has prospered, the lot of the servant woman has worsened.[49]

With a disturbing twist, the words of Sarah anticipate vocabulary and themes from the Exodus narrative. When plagues threatened the life of his firstborn son, Pharaoh cast out (*grš*) the Hebrew slaves.[50] Like that monarch, Sarah the matriarch wants to protect the life of her own son by casting out (*grš*) Hagar the slave. Having once fled from affliction (16:6b), Hagar continues to prefigure Israel's story even as Sarah foreshadows Egypt's role. Irony abounds.

According to the storyteller, Abraham disapproves of Sarah's order and so departs from his usual acquiescent role. His vision, however, encompasses only his son Ishmael. Hagar his wife he neglects altogether.

> The matter was very distressing (*r*ᶜᶜ)
> <u>in the eyes</u> of Abraham
> on account of (*'al 'ôdōt*) his son.
> (21:11)

Yet his resistance simply strengthens Sarah's power, for God sides with her. Consequently, the deity alters Abraham's vision.[51]

> Do not be distressed (*r*ᶜᶜ) <u>in your eyes</u>
> on account of (*'al*) the lad
> and on account of (*'al*) your slave woman.
> (21:12a)

Although most of this command repeats the narrated language, the changes merit attention. To minimize Abraham's relationship to Ishmael, God calls him "the lad" rather than "your son." Moreover, the deity describes Hagar not as "your wife" but as "your slave woman," a description that tellingly emulates the vocabulary of Sarah (21:10). If Abraham neglected Hagar, God belittles her.

In a second imperative, the deity explicitly confirms Sarah's order: "Everything that Sarah says to you, heed her voice" (21:12b; cf. 16:2).[52] A reason follows: "For in Isaac will be named to you descendants" (21:12c). In the midst of Sarah's triumph, the word *descendants* (zr^c) recalls Hagar's story. Long ago in the wilderness, the messenger of Yahweh said to her, "I will greatly multiply your descendants" (zr^c). That promise was made to Hagar alone, without reference to the father of her child (16:10). Juxtaposed, these two promises of progeny, first to Hagar through Ishmael and now to Abraham through Isaac, seem to allow Hagar the singular honor of being the female ancestor of a nation.[53] This interpretation falters, however, in light of God's closing words to Abraham:

> Also (*gam*) the son of the slave woman
> a nation I will make,
> for your descendant (zr^c) he is.
>
> (21:13)

The syntax of the sentence places object before verb, thereby highlighting the child of the slave woman. For Hagar, the apparent afterthought is devastating because it shifts descendants from her to Abraham. In various ways, then, Sarah, Abraham, God, and even Ishmael all diminish Hagar.

To protect the life of her own child, Sarah commands Abraham, "Cast out this slave woman and her son . . ." (21:10a). Supporting Sarah, God orders Abraham to obey. Though these instructions foreshadow themes and vocabulary of the Exodus story, the difference is again terrifying. When Pharaoh cast out (*grš*) the Hebrew slaves to save the life of his firstborn,[54] God was on their side to bring salvation from expulsion. By contrast, the deity identifies here not with the suffering slave but with her oppressors. Hagar knows banishment rather than liberation.

Abraham obeys Sarah and God to become the active agent in the suffering of Hagar (cf. 16:3, 6). The husband expels his slave wife and the father his son, although, in reporting these events, the narrator omits the relational ties. Abraham himself does not speak, but he does give bread and water to the outcasts. Such provisions suggest a precarious future for mother and child.

So Abraham rose early in the morning,[55]
and took bread and a skin of water
and gave it to Hagar, putting it on her
    shoulder, along with the child.[56]
        (21:14abc, RSV)

By using the name Hagar at the end of this episode, the storyteller matches the emphasis of the beginning (21:9). Abraham's last deed maintains this focus: "He sent her [not them] away" (21:14d, RSV). Like the verb *cast out*, this one (*send*) also anticipates vocabulary from the Exodus story, with a disturbing twist. As the act of Pharaoh, the verb *send away* (*šlḥ*) connotes freedom for the Hebrew slaves; as the act of Abraham, it means banishment for an Egyptian slave.[57] All the talk about Hagar has resulted in action against her. On this negative note, episode one concludes.

B. *Episode Two, 21:14e–19.* Though in scene one Hagar fled from Sarai, this time she has no escape. She must do what Sarah, God, and Abraham impose upon her. Their command determines her exit. "She departed" (21:14e) responds to the statement, "he sent her away" (21:14d).[58] Whereas in the Exodus traditions the verb *depart* (*hlk*), as the response to *send away* (*šlḥ*), describes what the Hebrews want to do,[59] in Hagar's story this corresponding action is what the slave woman must do. Identical words and similar themes tell opposing stories. Departing her land of bondage, Hagar knows not exodus but exile.

A second verb gives her destination: "She wandered in the wilderness of Beersheba" (21:14f, RSV*). In reference to physical movement, the verb *wander* (*tʿh*) connotes uncertainty, lack or loss of direction, and even destitution.[60] Since this word never describes the action of the Hebrews after the departure from Egypt, its use for Hagar indicates a wilderness experience different from theirs. Sent away from the land of bondage, "she departed and wandered in the wilderness. . . ." Through the pronoun *she*, Hagar becomes the subject of active verbs for the first time in this scene. If banishment is not liberation, nevertheless, it moves her toward personhood. The movement begins episode two.

In contrast to its parallel in scene one, this wilderness episode comprises two sections. The first (21:14e–16) depicts Hagar alone with her child; no divine messenger finds her by a spring of water.

In fact, unlike the region of Shur, the territory of Beersheba provides no water at all.[61] Furthermore, it does not border Egypt. Receiving Hagar in forced exile rather than voluntary flight, this wilderness is an arid and alien place. It offers a deathbed for the child.

> When the water in the skin was gone,
>   she left[62] the child under one of the bushes.
>   (21:15, RSV*)

Using "the child" (*yld*) rather than "her child" or "her son," the storyteller suggests emotional distance that becomes physical distance.

> Then she went and sat down over against him
>   a good way off, about the distance of a bowshot.[63]
>   (21:16a, RSV)

Unlike the bush (*sĕneh*) in the wilderness of Horeb (Exod. 3:2), the shrub (*śîaḥ*) under which the boy lies reveals no messenger of the Lord in a flame of fire.[64] In despair, Hagar contemplates the imminent death of the child. It is more than she can manage. For the only time in this entire scene, she speaks,[65] though her utterance is perhaps interior thought.[66] Deepening the portrait of this woman, the words suggest suffering and isolation in the wilderness of exile. "For she said, 'Let me not see (*r'h*) the death of the child'" (21:16b, RSV*). Having once seen (*r'h*) her conception of the child and also having seen (*r'h*) the God who sanctioned that new life (16:4, 13), the mother now seeks to block her vision of its demise. Like the narrator (21:15), she uses a vocabulary of distance. She speaks of "the child" rather than of "my child" or "my son." Directed to no one, these last words of Hagar surrender to death.

Hagar wept. Pointedly, the Hebrew text says, "She lifted up her voice and she wept" (21:16c). From ancient times, however, translators have robbed this woman of her grief by changing the unambiguous feminine verb forms to masculine constructions.[67] Such alterations make the child lift up his voice and weep. But masculine emendations cannot silence Hagar. A host of feminine verb forms throughout this section witness unmistakably to her tears: she departed and she wandered in the wilderness; she found a place for the child to die; she kept a vigil; and she uttered the dread phrase, "the death of the child." Now, as she sits at a distance from death, *she* lifts up her voice and *she* weeps. Her grief, like her speech, is sufficient unto itself. She does not cry out to another; she does not beseech God. A madonna alone with her dying child, Hagar weeps.

Of the few fragments that disclose Hagar's story, this section alone (21:14e–16) depicts her apart from all other major characters. Though the child is dying, the narrated focus remains steadily upon the mother: her actions, her thoughts, her words, her emotions. With one minor exception (21:15a), she is the subject of every verb. But her powerlessness is present in the absence of her name. Moreover, as subject she is also object, having been cast out into the wilderness. While the wilderness she chose in scene one was hospitable, yet fleeting, the wilderness imposed upon her in scene two is hostile, yet enduring. Thus this one symbol embodies for Hagar the polarities of life and death.

In time to come Israel will experience these polarities as its triumphal flight to freedom becomes forty years of life in the wilderness. Unlike Hagar, Israel will complain; it will murmur and rebel; it will demand food and water.[68] Yet throughout, God will be on Israel's side. With Hagar, the reverse happens. God supports, even orders, her departure to the wilderness, not to free her from bondage but to protect the inheritance of her oppressors.

If in the first section of this episode (21:14e–16) Hagar receives major attention, in the second (21:17–19) she begins to recede as the child comes to the forefront. God makes the difference. Narrated phrases at the ending and the beginning of the two sections signal the change. Hagar "lifted up her voice and wept" (21:16c) yields to "God heard the voice of the lad" (21:17a). A change in vocabulary from "the child" (*yld*) to "the lad" (*n'r*) also indicates this transition.

Although the mother's weeping elicits divine silence, the lad's voice evokes divine speech. But instead of finding Hagar in the wilderness (16:7), the messenger of God calls to her remotely "from heaven." As on the first occasion, the deity asks a question, addressing her by name: "What troubles you, Hagar?" (21:17c, RSV). Unlike the parallel occurrence (16:8), Hagar, the outcast rather than the fugitive, has no opportunity to reply. God continues to speak. Whereas in her exodus she answered the Lord, in her exile she

listens to a deity who is concerned primarily with her son: "Fear
not, for God has heard the voice of the lad where he is" (21:17d,
RSV).[69] When speaking to Hagar about her child, God never uses
the noun *son* or the adjective *your*. The deity follows the lead of the
narrator by referring to Ishmael as "the lad." Subtly, the motherhood of Hagar is undercut.

"Fear not, for God has heard the voice of the lad where he is."
This divine word of assurance confirms the shift from madonna to
child that the storyteller has introduced. In continuing, God exalts
"the lad" while making Hagar his support:

> Arise, lift up the lad
>   and hold him by your hand,
> for I shall make him a great nation.
>   (21:18, RSV*)

Unlike the revelation in scene one, the utterance contains no promises to Hagar (cf. 16:10). After all, the promise that *her* descendants
would be innumerable has already passed to Abraham (21:12–13),
and through him it comes to rest on the son. Hagar decreases as
Ishmael increases. Having lived under the hand of her mistress Sarai
(16:6, 9), this woman must now lift up the hand of "the lad."

Theophanic speech resolves the plight of the outcasts. In reporting
the aftermath, the narrator depicts the woman serving the child, as
God has decreed.

> Then God opened her eyes,
>   and she saw a well of water;
> and she went and filled the skin with water,
>   and she gave the lad a drink.
>   (21:19, RSV)

Once more visual language attends Hagar. At the beginning of this
episode, when the water in the skin was gone, she said, "Let me
not see (*r'h*) the death of the child" (21:16b, RSV*). Now, as God
opens her eyes, she sees (*r'h*) a well of water,[70] fills the skin, and
gives the lad a drink. Life overcomes death. Yet this language of
sight contrasts with the conclusion of Hagar's earlier sojourn in the
wilderness. On that occasion she was the theologian who named
Yahweh God of seeing (16:13). This time her voice ceases and her
vision changes. She sees not God but material resources to nourish

her child in the wilderness of exile.[71] From bondage to expulsion to homelessness, scene two brings Hagar's story to its close.

C. *Conclusion, 21:20–21.* Years pass with Hagar serving Ishmael. At first, the narrator credits only the deity.

> And God was with the lad;
> and he grew up and <u>lived in the wilderness,</u>
> and he became an expert with the bow.
>   (21:20, RSV*)

Ishmael prospers. For him the wilderness becomes home and provides work. To complete the picture, the storyteller turns from the providence of God to the activity of Hagar. For the last time she appears as a character in the Hebrew Bible,[72] and for the first time she is called mother. Yet Ishmael is still "the lad," not her son. Continuing to serve, the mother finds him a wife.

> <u>He lived in the wilderness</u> of Paran;[73]
> and his mother took for him a wife
> from the land of Egypt.
>   (21:21, RSV*)

The choice of a wife for Ishmael highlights tension in Hagar's story. Having at first promised her innumerable descendants (16:10), God later transferred that promise to Abraham (21:13). In her last act, Hagar guarantees that these descendants will be Egyptians.[74] Thus the mother suggests for herself a future that God has diminished. On this poignant note Hagar's story ends, but the reader's response does not.

REFLECTIONS ON HAGAR'S STORY

Belonging to a narrative that rejects her, Hagar is a fleeting yet haunting figure in scripture. To recover her story from the fragments that remain is a precarious task; nevertheless, it yields an abundance of hermeneutical reflections. In many and varied ways, Hagar shapes and challenges faith.

Read in light of contemporary issues and images, her story depicts oppression in three familiar forms: nationality, class, and sex.[75] Hagar the Egyptian is a maid; Sarah the Hebrew is her mistress. Conflicts between these two women revolve around three males. At the center is Abraham, their common husband. To him belong Ishmael, child of Hagar, and Isaac, child of Sarah. Through their husband and his two sons these females clash. From the beginning, however, Hagar is powerless because God supports Sarah. Kept in her place, the slave woman is the innocent victim of use, abuse, and rejection.[76]

As a symbol of the oppressed, Hagar becomes many things to many people. Most especially, all sorts of rejected women find their stories in her.[77] She is the faithful maid exploited, the black woman used by the male and abused by the female of the ruling class,[78] the surrogate mother, the resident alien without legal recourse, the other woman, the runaway youth, the religious fleeing from affliction, the pregnant young woman alone, the expelled wife, the divorced mother with child, the shopping bag lady carrying bread and water, the homeless woman, the indigent relying upon handouts from the power structures, the welfare mother, and the self-effacing female whose own identity shrinks in service to others.

Besides symbolizing various kinds and conditions of people in contemporary society, Hagar is a pivotal figure in biblical theology. She is the first person in scripture whom a divine messenger visits and the only person who dares to name the deity. Within the historical memories of Israel,[79] she is the first woman to bear a child. This conception and birth make her an extraordinary figure in the story of faith: the first woman to hear an annunciation, the only one to receive a divine promise of descendants, and the first to weep for her dying child. Truly, Hagar the Egyptian is the prototype of not only special but all mothers in Israel.[80]

Beyond these many distinctions, Hagar foreshadows Israel's pilgrimage of faith through contrast. As a maid in bondage, she flees from suffering. Yet she experiences exodus without liberation, revelation without salvation, wilderness without covenant, wanderings without land, promise without fulfillment, and unmerited exile without return.[81] This Egyptian slave woman is stricken, smitten by God, and afflicted for the transgressions of Israel. She is bruised for the iniquities of Sarah and Abraham; upon her is the chastisement that makes them whole.

Hagar is Israel, from exodus to exile, yet with differences. And these differences yield terror. All we who are heirs of Sarah and

Abraham, by flesh and spirit, must answer for the terror in Hagar's story. To neglect the theological challenge she presents is to falsify faith.[82]

NOTES

1. A correct understanding of this sentence depends upon its context. The phrase "within the confines of patriarchal structures" sharply curtails the privilege and power of Sarah. Further, such a description is contingent upon the contrast with Hagar and tempered by the fact of Sarai's barrenness. See note 17 below.

2. Wherever they are not identified in this essay, chapter and verse citations come from the book of Genesis.

3. I follow the biblical text in using two spellings for the names Sarai and Sarah; Abram and Abraham. On these variants, see the commentaries: e.g., Bruce Vawter, *On Genesis: A New Reading* (Garden City, N.Y.: Doubleday & Co., 1977), pp. 220, 223; E. A. Speiser, *Genesis*, Anchor Bible (Garden City, N.Y.: Doubleday & Co., 1964), p. 127; Gerhard von Rad, *Genesis*, OTL (Philadelphia: Westminster Press, 1972), pp. 199–200, 202. On the stigma of barrenness, see Phyllis Bird, "Images of Women in the Old Testament," in *Religion and Sexism*, ed. Rosemary Radford Ruether (New York: Simon & Schuster, 1974), pp. 62–63.

4. See Gen. 13:16; 15:4, 5.

5. Throughout this chapter the word *saga* means story.

6. Scholarly disciplines offer different readings of these stories. (a) Historical criticism attends to source analysis. Genesis 16:1–16 is J, with the exception of a few verses from P (16:1, 3, 15, 16), while Gen. 21:9–21 is E. See, e.g., S. R. Driver, *The Book of Genesis* (New York: Edwin S. Gorham, 1904), pp. 180–84, 209–13; Sean E. McEvenue, "A Comparison of Narrative Styles in the Hagar Stories," *Semeia* 3 (Missoula, Mont.: Scholars Press, 1975), pp. 64–80. For a revision of such analyses, see John Van Seters, *Abraham in History and Tradition* (New Haven, Conn.: Yale University Press, 1975), pp. 192–202; cf. also Alan W. Jenks, *The Elohist and North Israelite Traditions*, SBL Monograph Series 22 (Missoula, Mont.: Scholars Press, 1977), pp. 22, 67. (b) Form criticism attends to genre, oral traditions, settings in life, and literary parallels. See, e.g., Hermann Gunkel, *The Legends of Genesis* (New York: Schocken Books, 1964), *passim*; idem, *Genesis*, Handkommentar zum Alten Testament (Göttingen: Vandenhoeck & Ruprecht, 1964 reprint), pp. 184–93, 226–33; Robert C. Culley, *Studies in the Structure of Hebrew Narrative* (Philadelphia: Fortress Press, 1976), pp. 43–46; Hugh C. White, "The Initiation Legend of Ishmael," *ZAW* 87 (1975): 267–305. White also comments on the tradition history of the passage. Cf. Claus Westermann, *Genesis*, 2 Teilband, Biblischer Kommentar (Neukirchen-Vluyn: Neukirchener Verlag, 1981), pp. 281–82, 412–14. (c) As a development of form criticism, motif criticism attends to the identification and classification of plot-motifs and traditional episodes within the messenger stories. See Dorothy Irvin, *Mytharion* (Kevelaer: Butzon und

Bercker; Neukirchen-Vluyn: Neukirchener Verlag, 1978), pp. 1–17, 24–26. (d) Literary criticism attends to the type-scene as it moves between fixed conventions and flexible appropriations. See Robert Alter, *The Art of Biblical Narrative* (New York: Basic Books, 1981), pp. 47–62. Literary criticism also attends to close readings focused on the particularities of the text in its final form; cf. Zvi Adar, *The Biblical Narrative* (Jerusalem: Department of Education and Culture of the World Zionist Organisation, 1959), pp. 119–25. More than any other, this last approach shapes the present essay.

7. For a substantial bibliography, see the M.A. thesis of Bernadette F. Revicky, "'Hagar, Maidservant of Sarai, From What Place Have You Come and Where Shall You Go?': A Rhetorical Critical Study of Genesis 16 and Genesis 21:8–21," (M.A. thesis, Andover Newton Theological School, 1980), pp. 93–100.

8. Prepositional phrases side by side offer contrast and resolution. Although Sarai did not bear a child *to him* (*lô*), to her (*lāh*) was an Egyptian maid. The Egyptian identity of Hagar recalls the earlier sojourn of Abram and Sarai in Egypt (Gen. 12:10–20).

9. In Genesis 16, Hagar is identified as *šipḥâ*, a virgin, dependent maid who serves the mistress of the house, whereas in Genesis 21 she is called *'āmâ*, a slave woman who serves the master as a second wife. The latter term is the more oppressive. See A. Jepsen, "Amaʰ und Schiphchaʰ," *VT* 8 (1958): 293–97. To convey the distinction, I render *šipḥâ* as maid, servant, or bondswoman and *'āmâ* as slave. See Hans Walter Wolff, "Masters and Slaves," *Int* 27 (1973): 266–68; Westermann, *Genesis*, p. 283.

10. These are the first words of Sarai in the entire Abrahamic saga. On the importance of such speech, see Alter, *The Art of Biblical Narrative*, pp. 63–87. For the translation of *hinnēh-nā'* as *because* with the imperative (16:2a below), see Thomas O. Lambdin, *Introduction to Biblical Hebrew* (New York: Charles Scribner's Sons, 1971), pp. 170–71.

11. Cf. Gen. 30:1–13.

12. On the legalities of this arrangement, see, e.g., von Rad, *Genesis*, pp. 191–92; Speiser, *Genesis*, pp. 119–21; Vawter, *On Genesis*, pp. 214–15; Matitiahu Tsevat, "Hagar and the Birth of Ishmael," *The Meaning of the Book of Job and Other Biblical Studies* (New York: KTAV Publishing House, 1980), pp. 53–76. But also cf. John Van Seters, "The Problem of Childlessness in Near Eastern Law and the Patriarchs of Israel," *JBL* 87 (1968): 401–8; Thomas L. Thompson, *The Historicity of the Patriarchal Narratives* (Berlin: Walter de Gruyter, 1974), pp. 252–69. On this issue in the context of current research on the patriarchal narratives, see William G. Denver [*sic*] and W. Malcolm Clark, "The Patriarchal Traditions," *Israelite and Judean History*, ed. John H. Hayes and J. Maxwell Miller (Philadelphia: Westminster Press, 1977), pp. 70–148; M. J. Selman, "Comparative Customs and the Patriarchal Age," *Essays on the Patriarchal Narratives*, ed. A. R. Millard and D. J. Wiseman (Winona Lake, Ind.: Eisenbrauns, 1983), pp. 91–139.

13. Drawing upon cognate languages and legal background, some scholars do render *'iššâ* here as concubine rather than wife (e.g., Speiser, *Genesis*, pp. 116–17; Vawter, *Genesis*, pp. 213–14). But cf. RSV and Westermann,

Genesis, p. 277. The specific Hebrew word for concubine (*pilegeš*) does not appear in Hagar's story; cf. Judg. 19:1.

14. Like Sarai, Abram never uses the name Hagar nor does he speak to her; only narration reports the direct contact between them (16:4; 21:14).

15. Cf. von Rad, *Genesis*, pp. 190–91; Vawter, *On Genesis*, pp. 214–15; Westermann, *Genesis*, pp. 286–87.

16. Cf. Rachel and Leah (Gen. 30:1); Hannah and Peninnah (1 Sam. 1:4–6). Of special interest also is the rivalry between Hebrew and Egyptian women during the Exodus period (Exod. 1:19). In our story, the contrast between bonded and free, foreign and native women reverses to oppose the fertile Egyptian maid to the barren Hebrew mistress. On such rivalry as a plot-motif, see Irvin, *Mytharion*, pp. 15, 17.

17. Cf. Prov. 30:21–23. Recall that Sarai, as well as Hagar, is a victim of patriarchy (see note 1). On infighting among oppressed groups, see Paulo Freire, *Pedagogy of the Oppressed* (New York: Continuum, 1983), p. 48. Cf. Rosemary Radford Ruether, *Sexism and God-Talk* (Boston: Beacon Press, 1983), pp. 165–83.

18. Tsevat understands Sarai's words to constitute a legal form ("Hagar and the Birth of Ishmael," p. 55); cf. Westermann, *Genesis*, p. 287.

19. Cf. Vawter's gentle treatment of Abram over against his harsh judgment of Sarai (*On Genesis*, p. 215).

20. E.g., Exod. 1:11, 12; Deut. 26:6; cf. Gen. 15:13. See David Daube, *The Exodus Pattern in the Bible* (London: Faber & Faber, 1963), pp. 26–27.

21. On Shur, see Denis Baly and A. D. Tushingham, *Atlas of the Biblical World* (New York: World Publishing Company, 1971), p. 104, and J. Simons, *The Geographical and Topographical Texts of the Old Testament* (Leiden: E. J. Brill, 1959), p. 217. Cf. Gen. 20:1; 25:18; 1 Sam. 15:7; 27:8.

22. Moses' flight from Pharaoh (Exod. 2:15b) and Hagar's flight from Sarai employ the same verb (*brḥ*). After fleeing, Moses "sat down by a well" (Exod. 2:15c); Hagar was "by a spring of water in the wilderness" (Gen. 16:7).

23. See Martin Buber, *On the Bible* (New York: Schocken Books, 1968), p. 39. On the messenger of God, see Westermann, *Genesis*, pp. 289–91. Whether or not Hagar immediately recognizes the divine messenger is uncertain; see Tsevat, "Hagar and the Birth of Ishmael," pp. 56–57, 64.

24. Note that the direct speeches of all the other characters are repeatedly introduced by their proper names even when such identifications are unnecessary (16:2, 5, 6, 9, 10, 11). For other instances of the correlation between the presence of name and speech and the phenomenon of personhood, see the comments on Tamar in chapter 2; see also, on the book of Ruth, Phyllis Trible, *God and the Rhetoric of Sexuality* (Philadelphia: Fortress Press, 1978), pp. 166–70, 190.

25. Tsevat also notes affinities between this story and the Exodus tradition, but with a different interpretation ("Hagar and the Birth of Ishmael," p. 69).

26. Historical, form, and redaction critics tend to separate these promises by appeals to earlier forms of the text. Their conclusions are often contradictory. See, e.g., Vawter, *On Genesis*, p. 217; Van Seters, *Abraham in*

History and Tradition, pp. 194–95; Claus Westermann, *The Promises to the Fathers* (Philadelphia: Fortress Press, 1980), pp. 12–13; idem, *Genesis*, pp. 292–95; Robert Wilbur Neff, "The Announcement in Old Testament Birth Stories" (Ph.D. diss., Yale University, 1969), pp. 97–102; Tsevat, "Hagar and the Birth of Ishmael," pp. 57–60. My concern is the coherence of the final form of the text.

27. E.g., Gen. 15:5; 22:17; 26:4; 28:3. Note that the term "your descendants" (*zrᶜ*) refers not to the seed of Abram, even though he is the biological father, but rather to the offspring of Hagar; cf. Gen. 3:15 where *zrᶜ* again specifies the "seed" of the woman rather than of the man.

28. *Contra* Van Seters who finds 16:10 incompatible with 16:11 (*Abraham in History and Tradition*, p. 194).

29. For a form-critical analysis, see Neff, "The Announcement in Old Testament Birth Stories," pp. 55–69, 104–8; also Robert Wilbur Neff, "The Annunciation in the Birth Narrative of Ishmael," *BR* 17 (1972): 51–60.

30. Of the six birth announcements studied by Neff (Gen. 16:11–12; Gen. 17:19; Judg. 13:5, 7; 2 Kings 13:2; 2 Chron. 22:9–10; Isa. 7:14–17), only two (Gen. 16:11–12 and Judg. 13:5, 7) are spoken directly to women (Hagar and Ms. Manoah). Cf. also the Shunammite woman in 2 Kings 4:16; note that the prophet Elisha, not a divine figure, speaks to her. In the New Testament a birth announcement is spoken directly to Mary (Luke 1:26–38); cf. the announcement to Zechariah about Elizabeth (Luke 1:13–20).

31. For discussions of the name Ishmael, see Mitchell Dahood, "The Name *yišmāᶜēl* in Genesis 16, 11," *Biblica* 49 (1968): 87–88; idem, "Nomen-Omen in Genesis 16, 11," *Biblica* 61 (1980): 89. Cf. Irvin, *Mytharion*, p. 15.

32. The theme of deliverance from the afflictions in Egypt echoes in the line, "Yahweh has paid heed (*šmᶜ*) to your affliction (*ᶜŏnî*);" cf. Deut. 26:7. On this and other wordplays in the story, see Martin Buber, *Darko shel miqra* (Jerusalem: Bialik Institute, 1964), pp. 295–97.

33. See Tsevat, "Hagar and the Birth of Ishmael," p. 67.

34. The pointing of the Hebrew text allows two meanings for this declaration: the God who may be seen and the God who sees (me). Though the Greek Bible and the Vulgate choose the second, the ambiguity of the MT is perhaps desirable to retain. See John Skinner, *A Critical and Exegetical Commentary on Genesis*, ICC (Edinburgh: T. & T. Clark, 1930), p. 288; Speiser, *Genesis*, p. 118.

35. Note that her declaration of divine seeing, with its positive emphasis, occurs after the birth announcement, not after the divine command to submit to affliction. Cf. Hagar's plight with that of the Hebrew slaves who were delivered from their affliction because God saw (*r'h*) it (Exod. 3:7).

36. On auditory versus visual speech in Old Testament theophanies, see Samuel Terrien, *The Elusive Presence* (New York: Harper & Row, 1978), *passim*.

37. Cf. Speiser, *Genesis*, pp. 117–19.

38. Attempting to connect Hagar's words with the aetiological note that follows them, Julius Wellhausen emended the text in several ways to have Hagar ask, "Have I really seen God and yet remained alive?" (*Prolegomena to the History of Ancient Israel* [New York: Meridian Library, 1958], p.

326). Cf. Skinner, *Genesis*, pp. 288–89; Tsevat, "Hagar and the Birth of Ishmael," pp. 63, 66; Westermann, *Genesis*, pp. 296–97. Though such a question has a theological base in the assertion that no person may see the deity and live (cf. Exod. 33:20; Judg. 6:23; 13:20–23) and also offers another foreshadowing of an Exodus motif in Hagar's story, nevertheless, the reading remains an emendation. Cf. H. Seebass, "Zum Text Von Gen. XVI 13B," *VT* (1971): 254–56; Irvin, *Mytharion*, p. 16 and the references cited there; Neff, "The Announcement in Old Testament Birth Stories," pp. 93–94; Th. Booij, "Hagar's Words in Genesis XVI 13B," *VT* 30 (1980): 1–7; A. Schoors, "A *Tiqqun Sopherim* in Genesis XVI 13B?" *VT* 32 (1982): 494–95.

39. Note the use of repetitions with variations. They enclose the unit as well as mark emphases within it.

40. Note the possessive "his son" as well as the repeated assertion that the child was born to Abram; cf. Gen. 25:9, 12.

41. Cf. Robert Alter, "How Convention Helps Us Read: The Case of the Bible's Annunciation Type-Scene," *Prooftexts* 3 (1983): 115–30, especially 120–21. In light of his proposed schema for the annunciation type-scene, Alter is unable to take account of the birth announcement to Hagar.

42. See Robert Wilbur Neff, "The Birth and Election of Isaac in the Priestly Tradition," *BR* 15 (1970): 5–18.

43. Cf. Isaac Rabinowitz, "Sarah's Wish (Gen. XXI 6–7)," *VT* 29 (1979): 362–63.

44. The Greek Bible says that he was "playing with Isaac." This reading has prompted different interpretations: e.g., that Ishmael was physically abusing Isaac; that the social equality implied between the two children was unacceptable to Sarah. When the phrase "with Isaac" is omitted, other interpretations follow: e.g., that Ishmael was masturbating; that his joyous demeanor aroused Sarah's maternal jealousy (Jubilees 17:4). See the commentaries, e.g., Driver, *The Book of Genesis*, p. 155; Vawter, *On Genesis*, pp. 248–49; von Rad, *Genesis*, p. 232; Westermann, *Genesis*, pp. 414–15. Note that the verb *play* (*ṣḥq*) suggests a pun on the name Isaac (*yiṣḥāq*).

45. On the legalities involved, see Nahum M. Sarna, *Understanding Genesis* (New York: McGraw-Hill, 1966), pp. 155–57; Thompson, *The Historicity of the Patriarchal Narratives*, pp. 257–58.

46. The name Ishmael never occurs in scene two.

47. Another sign of the increased distance between Sarah and Hagar, in contrast to episode one of scene one (16:3), is the absence of any direct contact between them.

48. See note 9 above; also Westermann, *Genesis*, p. 415.

49. Cf. the comments above on 16:4.

50. Exod. 12:39; cf. 6:1; 10:11; 11:1. See Daube, *The Exodus Pattern in the Bible*, pp. 30–34.

51. Note the repeated use of the idiom "in . . . eyes" by the narrator, Sarai, Abram, and the deity (16:4, 5, 6; 21:11).

52. Note that in 21:12–13 God also "heeds the voice" of Sarah by emulating her vocabulary of 21:10: the use of the name *Isaac* (v. 12) and not the names *Hagar* and *Ishmael*; the use of *slave woman* (vv. 12, 13) and of *son* (v. 13). Von Rad calls vv. 12–13 the "'tense moment' in the structure

of the narrative'' because the reader expects God to be on the side of Abraham, not of Sarah (*Genesis*, p. 233).

53. Note the similarities in form and content, as well as the divergencies in meaning, between the opening sections of this episode (21:9–12) and the corresponding material in 16:1–2: (a) Narrated introductions set up tension between the two women (16:1; 21:9). (b) With direct discourse, Sarai (Sarah) commands Abram (Abraham) to act upon Hagar. In the first imperative (16:2a), Sarai wants to obtain a son through Hagar; in the second (21:10), she wants that son, along with Hagar, sent away from her. (c) Different narrated responses by Abram yield different results. The first time he obeys Sarai (16:2b), and the episode continues without intervention by the deity. The second time (21:11) Abraham balks, and so God enters to assure that Sarah's will be done (21:12).

54. See Exod. 6:1; 10:11; 12:39 for uses of the verb *cast out* (*grš*).

55. For the phrase ''rose early in the morning'' as a formula to introduce a unit of action, see Irvin, *Mytharion*, p. 25.

56. On the syntactical problems of the Hebrew text, see Speiser, *Genesis*, p. 155; Vawter, *On Genesis*, p. 249.

57. On uses of *šlḥ* in the Exodus story, see Daube, *The Exodus Pattern in the Bible*, p. 29. He suggests that the banishment of Hagar by Abraham constitutes a divorce.

58. These geographical and pronominal changes indicate that a new section of the story begins with 21:14b, *contra* many translations (e.g., RSV, NEB, NAB, and NJV).

59. On the pairing of *send away* (*šlḥ*) and *depart* (*hlk*), see Daube, *The Exodus Pattern in the Bible*, p. 34; cf. pp. 58–59.

60. See, e.g., Gen. 37:15; Ps. 107:4; 119:176; Isa. 53:6; Job 38:41.

61. On the ''wilderness of Beersheba,'' see the entry ''Desert'' in Simons, *The Geographical and Topographical Texts of the Old Testament*, pp. 21–23.

62. With the NJV, I translate the verb *šlk* as *left* to distinguish it from the verb *grš* (*cast*) in 21:10; *contra* RSV.

63. The reference to ''bowshot'' foreshadows the description of Ishmael as an ''expert with the bow'' (21:20).

64. *Contra* Gunkel, the shrub is not a holy place (*Genesis*, pp. 230–31). The deity speaks to Hagar explicitly ''from heaven'' (21:17).

65. In both scenes Hagar speaks in the wilderness and not in the house of Abraham and Sarah.

66. On interior thought, see Alter, *The Art of Biblical Narrative*, pp. 69–70.

67. This change appears first in the Greek Bible; cf. RSV, NAB. For attempts to justify the change, see, e.g., Skinner, *Genesis*, pp. 248–49. But cf. Speiser, *Genesis*, pp. 155–56.

68. See George W. Coats, *Rebellion in the Wilderness* (Nashville: Abingdon Press, 1968).

69. Cf. the play on the name Ishmael. For a form-critical study of this divine speech, see Westermann, *Genesis*, p. 419.

70. See Westermann, *Genesis*, p. 420.

71. Certain themes and vocabulary suggest associations between this text

and Gen. 22:1–19. In both stories two sons of Abraham are under threat of death; at the crucial moment the deity intervenes to spare the children. God opens the *eyes* of Hagar; she sees (*r'h*) a well of water and gives the lad a drink (21:19). Abraham lifts up his *eyes*, sees (*r'h*) a ram that the Lord has provided (*r'h*), and sacrifices it instead of his son (22:13–14). Note also the repeated use of phrases and words, such as "Abraham rose early in the morning" (21:14; 22:3); "angel of God (Lord) called to . . . from heaven" (21:17; 22:11); "fear" (*yr'*, 21:17; 22:12); "the lad" (21:17, 18, 20; 22:5, 12); "hand" (21:18; 22:10, 12). Cf. Alter, *The Art of Biblical Narrative*, pp. 181–82. Similar geographical settings may also relate these stories; see Baly and Tushingham, *Atlas of the Biblical World*, p. 104. For a meditation, see Arthur I. Waskow, "The Cloudy Mirror: Ishmael and Isaac," *Godwrestling* (New York: Schocken Books, 1978), pp. 23–33.

72. Though reference is made to Hagar in the genealogical list of Gen. 25:12, she herself does not appear as a character.

73. On Paran, see Baly and Tushingham, *Atlas of the Biblical World*, pp. 93, 104; Simons, *The Geographical and Topographical Texts of the Old Testament*, p. 22.

74. Cf. the ancient Near Eastern custom of the father securing a wife for his son (Speiser, *Genesis*, p. 156). Note the continuing emphasis on the Egyptian theme in the genealogical introduction of Gen. 25:12 as well as in the geographical reference to Shur opposite Egypt (25:18; cf. 16:7).

75. I use the word *sex* to designate people, female and male. The word *gender* I reserve for grammar. See William Safire, "On Language: Vox of Pop Sixpack," *The New York Times Magazine*, 19 December 1982, pp. 18–19.

76. Recent studies on the interrelationships of racism, classism, and sexism are pertinent here; cf. e.g., Rosemary Radford Ruether, *New Woman/New Earth* (New York: Seabury Press, 1975), pp. 115–33; Adrienne Rich, *On Lies, Secrets, and Silence: Selected Prose 1966–1978* (New York: W. W. Norton & Co., 1979), pp. 275–310.

77. The list that follows reflects stories of contemporary women who identify with Hagar. Cf. Margaret Laurence, *The Stone Angel* (Toronto: McClelland & Stewart, 1968).

78. While racial ties between the ancient Egyptians and black people are problematic, cultural affinities are certain. Hagar was an African woman. On this issue in general, see Robert A. Bennett, Jr., "Africa and the Biblical Period," *HTR* 64 (1971): 483–500.

79. By historical memories, I mean to exclude Genesis 1—11.

80. See Zvi Adar, *The Biblical Narrative*, p. 124.

81. In light of these contrasts, note the irony of Paul's equating Hagar with the Sinai covenant (Gal. 4:21–31). Cf. Walter Brueggemann, *Genesis*, Interpretation (Atlanta: John Knox Press, 1982), p. 184.

82. The place of Hagar in Islam also deserves mention. She does not appear in the Qur'ān but in the *Hadiths*; see Arendt Jan Wensinck, *A Handbook of Early Muhammedan Tradition* (Leiden: E. J. Brill, 1960), p. 90.

TAMAR

Princess of Judah

A woman of sorrows
and acquainted
with grief.

CHAPTER 2

Tamar

The Royal Rape of Wisdom

2 Samuel 13:1–22

From the book of Samuel comes the story of a family enmeshed in royal rape. Brother violates sister. He is a prince to whom belong power, prestige, and unrestrained lust. She is a princess to whom belong wisdom, courage, and unrelieved suffering. Children of one father, they have not the same care of each other. Indeed, the brother cares not at all.

Though part of a narrative about King David and his court, this tale of terror stands on its own.[1] Within a well-ordered design the plot moves from obstacles and plans to the crime and its aftermath. Three episodes (A, B, C) lead to the rape (D) and three follow from it (B', C', A'). Our task is to explore the artistry and meaning of this literary unit as we attend to its single female character.[2]

BEFORE THE CRIME, 13:1–9c[3]

In preparation for the crime, episode one presents the characters and their circumstances; episode two reports a scheme devised for the prince by his advisor; and episode three enlists the authority of the king. Circular structures organize these first two units while the third builds on a chain of command and response.

A. *Introduction: Characters and Circumstances, 13:1–3.* The story commences with a transitional phrase, "And it came to pass after this." Behind lie the sordid deeds of David to secure Bathsheba, the redeeming birth of his son Solomon, and a decisive victory over the Ammonites. The king has enjoyed success in all things public and private. But now the narrator leaves these exploits. To be sure,

David alone survives from the preceding scenes, yet in a subordinate role. He is a member of the supporting cast.

Following the transitional phrase, a ring composition introduces the characters around a description of circumstances (13:1–3).[4] Within this structure, circular patterns reflect the whole. At the beginning come three children of David.[5] First named is Absalom, the third son, whose presence hovers over the entire tale, though he himself appears only near the end. Last is Amnon, the firstborn, whose desire initiates the action. Between these two males stands the female who relates to each of them and also has her own identity. Sister to Absalom and object of desire to Amnon, this beautiful woman is Tamar. The circular arrangement of the verse centers upon her:

> To Absalom, son of David,
>   a sister beautiful, with the name Tamar,
> and desired her Amnon, son of David.
>   (13:1)

Two males surround a female. As the story unfolds, they move between protecting and polluting, supporting and seducing, comforting and capturing her. Further, these sons of David compete with each other through the beautiful woman.

For a time, the narrator puts Absalom aside to develop the latter half of the circle, "And desired her Amnon, son of David."[6] The information leads to the center of the episode, a description of circumstances that bode trouble (13:2). "So tormented was Amnon that he made himself ill on account of Tamar his sister" (13:2a, RSV*). Although first linked to the crown prince solely as object of desire, Tamar receives here the designation "his sister." The word relating her to Absalom also binds her to Amnon. The storyteller has chosen to stress familial ties, for such intimacy exacerbates the coming tragedy.[7]

This sibling connection, however, is not the reason for Amnon's frustration and illness. His passion is pain "because a virgin was she, and it was impossible in the eyes of Amnon to do to her anything" (13:2b). Full of lust, the prince is impotent; full of sight, he lacks insight. As a virgin, Tamar is protected property, inaccessible to males, including her brother. Yet the ominous phrase, "it was impossible . . . to do to her anything," not only underscores his frustration but also foreshadows the disaster of its release.[8] Explicating the meaning of Amnon's desire, lust-sickness and violent yearning enclose the virgin:

> So tormented was <u>Amnon</u> that he made himself ill
> on account of Tamar his sister,
>
> for a virgin was she,
>
> and it was impossible in the eyes of <u>Amnon</u>
> to do to her anything.
>
> (13:2)

If in the first circle (13:1) the two brothers surrounding Tamar contrast helping and harming her, in the second circle one brother signifies total danger. In fact, the inhibition of violence leads to its opposite. Though Amnon finds it "impossible to do to her anything," a perspective and a plan come from someone else. Jonadab is that person.

As the conclusion to episode one, the introduction of Jonadab completes a ring composition:

> To Amnon a friend with the name Jonadab,
> son of Shimeah, brother of David.
> Jonadab was a very crafty man.
>
> (13:3)

At the beginning of the unit (13:1a), a prepositional phrase followed by a noun joined two people: "to (*lĕ*) Absalom . . . a sister." Then came her personal identity: "with the name Tamar." Now at the end is a parallel structure: "To (*lĕ*) Amnon a friend with the name Jonadab." Attached to the name is the identification, "son of Shimeah, brother of David." Jonadab is a cousin in the royal family. Like the king's sons, he relates explicitly to David and thus acquires a status never granted Tamar the daughter. Moreover, a juxtaposition of adjectives shows Jonadab's advantage over Tamar. Although she is "beautiful (*yph*)," Jonadab is "very crafty (*ḥkm*)."[9] His entrance gives Amnon the friend he needs to surmount the impossible. This pair contrasts with Tamar and Absalom. At the same time, the parallelism falters, for Tamar alone is the object and potential victim of lust. In the beginning, two brothers surround her; in the middle, sickness and contemplated violence entrap her; in the end, the very crafty Jonadab surpasses her. Truly, episode one portends disaster for Tamar.

B. *Jonadab and Amnon, 13:4–5.* From narrated discourse the story moves to a conversation between Jonadab and Amnon. Commencing with questions and closing with instructions, the crafty friend envelops the lustful prince in solicitude and advice. First, he provokes an explanation of Amnon's condition.[10]

> Why are you so haggard, son of the king,
>   morning after morning?
> Will you not tell me?
>
> (13:4, RSV*)

Focusing upon royal as well as familial status, the vocative, "son of the king," heightens incongruity. Surely the heir apparent need not be weak, thin, haggard, or impoverished.[11]

Jonadab's approach succeeds, for Amnon answers forthrightly. "Tamar, sister-of Absalom, my-brother, I desire" (13:4). Syntax and vocabulary yield a well-constructed sentence of six Hebrew words. Tamar, the object of the verb, comes first, for she is his obsession. The remaining words are striking in their alliteration. Each begins with the letter *aleph*, giving the impression, perhaps, of halting sighs. Yet only at the end does Amnon reveal his yearning. "I (*'ănî*)," he says emphatically, "desire (*'hb*)." Hence, the beginning and end of this sentence match the report that "her name was Tamar and desired (*'hb*) her Amnon, son of David" (13:1). Narrator and character seem to tell the same tale.

But the middle words of the confession alter this continuity: "sister-of Absalom, my-brother." For the first time, fraternal language enters to indicate friction between the royal sons. The designation, "sister-of Absalom," supports this tension while deflecting Tamar's kinship to Amnon (cf. 13:2). The entire phrase implies a different obstacle from the narrated explanation. According to Amnon, Absalom, not virginity, stands between the object and his desire. If this male can be removed, the female becomes accessible. "Tamar, sister-of Absalom, my-brother, *I* desire," says Amnon to Jonadab. In this speech-event converge the four characters whom the storyteller has juxtaposed (cf. 13:1, 3). Again, their pairing is uneven.

Absalom and Tamar are the objects of discourse; Jonadab and Amnon plot against them.

"And Jonadab said to him [Amnon], 'Lie upon your bed and act ill'" (13:5). In Hebrew the first verb and object share the same root (*škb*), thereby introducing a key word: "Lie upon your lying-place." The second imperative, "act ill," exploits Amnon's condition. Though he has made himself genuinely sick (*ḥlh*) on account of Tamar (13:2), Jonadab recommends that he feign illness (*ḥlh*) to provoke a paternal visit.[12] In addition, he tells Amnon what to say.

> When your father comes to see you,
>   then you say to him,
> "Let come Tamar my sister
>   and let her feed me food
>   and let her do before my eyes the food
>   so that I may see
>   and eat from her hand."
> (13:5b)

With attention to detail, the plan emerges. Amnon should use the coming (*bô'*) of his father to request the coming (*bô'*) of *his* sister, not Absalom's sister. To claim kinship with Tamar this time averts suspicion (cf. 13:4). Moreover, her visit should be lengthy. Not only would she, like a nurse, give Amnon food, but also, like a maid, she would prepare the food before his eyes, thus feeding the lust of sight. The phrase, "let her do (*'śh*) before my eyes the food," recalls the impossibility "in the eyes of Amnon to do (*'śh*) to her anything" (13:2). While the feeding and preparing of food occur in reverse order, the consequences come in proper sequence: "that I may see and eat from her hand."[13] The lack of an object for the verb *see* poses shrewd ambiguity.[14] Though David must be made to think that Amnon wants to see the food being prepared, the reader knows that he wants to see Tamar. Further, to "eat from her hand" would bring her within grasp.

Jonadab is indeed cunning.[15] Having elicited from Amnon a confession that seeks license, he schemes to gratify the prince. The skills of a counselor he employs to promote illness. He would use the father to overcome the obstacle of the brother and secure the sister. Around Amnon, then, his speeches weave a net of friendship that ensnares Tamar, Absalom, and David. With its own ring structure, this second episode bears emphatically the message of the first: Tamar is trapped.

C. *David and His Children, 13:6–9c.* From description (episode one) and advice (episode two), the story moves to action. In episode three, circular patterns yield to linear progressions that, nevertheless, begin and end at Amnon's house. The verbs *coming* (*bô'*; 13:6), *sending* (*šlḥ*; 13:7), and *going* (*hlk*; 13:7, 8) signal the movement of plot and place. Unlike the preceding episodes, this one mixes narrated and direct discourse. Storyteller and characters unite to continue the tale.

The scheme of Jonadab pivots on David. "Amnon lay down (*škb*) and acted ill and the king came to see him" (13:6a). Breaking with the vocabulary of Jonadab to identify David as monarch rather than father, the narrator accents authority without power. The king bows to the prince. So Amnon speaks, appropriating the words of Jonadab.[16]

> Let come Tamar my sister.
> Let her make bread (*lbb*) before my eyes,
>   a couple of cakes,
>   that I may eat (*brh*) from her hand.
>   (13:6b)

A special verb for making bread (*lbb*) appears here. It suggests in Hebrew a play upon the word *heart*, and the pun fits the occasion.[17] Tamar preparing the desired bread will herself be the desire of Amnon's heart. Feasting upon her with his eyes, his lust will reach out to eat from her hand.

The son's request becomes the king's order. Immediately David sends (*šlḥ*) word to Tamar at the house. Though "the king" visited Amnon, "David" dispatches a message to Tamar. No familial language relates father and daughter—only two commands that impel disaster (13:7). First, "Go to the house of Amnon your brother." The fraternal reference would seem to guarantee safety. Second, "Make for him the food." The imperative *make* or *do* (*'śh*) hints that it is no longer impossible for Amnon to do (*'śh*) anything to his virgin sister (cf. 13:2, 5). Unwittingly, David has sealed Tamar's fate.[18]

From Jonadab to Amnon to David to Tamar the story develops, with increasing speed and varying nuances, from advice to request to command to obedience.[19] With Tamar, the parade of characters stops, and the chain of action holds. Direct discourse ceases. The narrator heightens suspense by concentrating upon the young woman. "So Tamar went (*hlk*) to the house of Amnon her brother" (13:8a, RSV*). A parenthetical observation intervenes to continue an ironic play on the verb *lie* (*škb*; cf. 13:5, 6). "Now he was lying down" (13:8b). Amnon's supine position becomes a posture of power devastating for Tamar. So the attention returns to her. Six verbs, in sets of threes, detail her activities. They focus on Amnon's eyes:

> She took the dough
> > and she kneaded it
> > and she made bread (*lbb*)
> > > *before his eyes*;
> > and she baked the bread (*lbbt*)[20]
> > and she took the pan
> > and she served
> > > before him.
> > > > (13:8c–9b)

In obeying David, Tamar has become the object of sight. Amnon, the narrator, and the readers behold her. Voyeurism prevails.[21] Yet Amnon himself wants more than illicit sight; he desires forbidden flesh. Abruptly, he "refuses to eat" (13:9c). All that his lust demands he must have, and refusal is his way to fulfillment. The prince has duped the king; the princess must suffer the consequences. Thus the story moves to its center.

THE CRIME: AMNON AND TAMAR, 13:9d–18

In this central unit,[22] form and content yield a flawed chiasmus that embodies irreparable damage for the characters. Amnon's commands and various responses to them mark the beginning and the end.[23] Within the *inclusio* Amnon and Tamar are the sole participants. In the first half come his command and her response, followed by a conversation between the two. In the corresponding section of the second half, their conversation collapses into his command and her response.[24] The rape itself constitutes the center of the chiasmus.[25] This design verifies the message of the preceding circular patterns:[26] Tamar is entrapped for rape.

a   Amnon's command to the servants and their response (13:9de)
  b   Amnon's command to Tamar and her response (13:10–11a)
    c   Conversation between Amnon and Tamar (13:11b–14a)
      d   Rape (13:14b–15b)
    c'-b'   Conversation between Amnon and Tamar:
      Amnon's command to Tamar and her response (13:15c–16)
a'   Amnon's command to a servant and his response (13:17–18)

(a) "Go out (*yṣ'*), every man, from me," orders Amnon (13:9d). His command is obeyed in identical language. "And they went out (*yṣ'*), every man, from him" (13:9e). Though all witnesses apparently leave, the narrator remains to see evil unfold and record its aftermath for the reader.[27] Amnon's power to banish all has its limits.

(b) Alone with Tamar, the prince addresses her for the first time but fails to use her name. "Bring the food (*bryh*) to the bedroom that I may eat from your hand" (13:10a).[28] What his eyes have possessed, his hand seeks to hold. Moving Tamar into the bedroom of the house (13:8) reinforces the planned intimacy.

The princess who once obeyed the king is the sister heeding Amnon's instructions. She ministers to a sick and deceiving brother. Not a word does she speak. Three main verbs describe her actions: take, bring, and give. The first verb parallels earlier deeds. "Tamar took (*lqḥ*) the bread," even as she had taken (*lqḥ*) the dough and then the pan (13:8). Parenthetically, this bread is the desired food (*lbbt*) "which she had made" (*'śh*; 13:10b). As she has "done" (*'śh*) the bread before the eyes of Amnon, so it becomes possible for him to "do" (*'śh*) something to her (cf. 13:2). "Tamar took the bread which she had made." If the verb *take* alludes to her past actions, the verb *bring* responds to present orders: "She brought [the bread] to Amnon her brother to his bedroom" (13:10c).[29] The third action, in the privacy of the bedroom, leads her directly to Amnon. "She gave to him to eat" (13:11a). The time for violence is at hand.

(c) "He grabbed hold (*ḥzq*) of her" (13:11b).[30] Quick and forceful action precedes a crude invitation for rape. "Come, lie (*škb*) with

me, my sister" (13:11c, RSV).[31] Through a series of orders, all of
them obeyed, Amnon has manipulated the occasion to feed his lust.
This time, however, the royal command meets objection. In the
presence of a rapist, Tamar panics not. In fact, she claims her voice.
Unlike Amnon's brisk commands, her deliberations slow the movement of the plot, though they are unable to divert it.[32] If Amnon
used the vocative to seduce her, she returns it to summon him to
sense:[33]

> No ('al), my brother.
> (13:12a, RSV)

Negatives persist:

> Do not ('al) violate ('nh) me,
>   for (kî) it is not (lōʾ) done thus in Israel.
> (13:12bc, RSV*)

Her appeal is to the custom of their people, not to divine law or
inner feelings. Repeating the key verb *do*, the last negative accents
the point:

> Do not ('al) do ('śh) this foolish thing.[34]
> (13:12d, RSV*)

Turning from prohibition, Tamar pursues the folly of Amnon's
demand. Carefully she weighs the consequences in a rhetorical question about herself and a projected description of her brother:

> I ('ănî), where would I carry my shame?
> You ('attāh), you would be like one of
>   the fools in Israel.
> (13:13ab)

Unrestrained, Amnon's desire means disaster for them both. Hence,
Tamar seeks an alternative. The solution lies with David, the highest
human authority in the realm. Referring to him as monarch, Tamar
sets distance between father and daughter:

> Now speak to the king,
>   for (kî) he will not keep me from you.
> (13:13c, RSV*)

Her words are honest and poignant; they acknowledge female servitude. Tamar knows Amnon can have her but pleads that he do it

properly.[35] Though Jonadab advised Amnon to seek David's help, how different was that counsel. Over against Jonadab stands Tamar. Wisdom opposes craftiness. In light of her words, not only Amnon but also Jonadab is a fool. Yet in this story victory belongs to the fools.

Precisely now, when Tamar speaks for the first time, the narrator hints at her powerlessness by avoiding her name. Repeatedly, the introductions to direct speeches of male characters use their proper names: Jonadab said, Amnon said, David said, and Absalom said. Such a pattern occurs even where the pronoun *he* would suffice (e.g., 13:6c, 10, 15c). By contrast, the name Tamar never prefaces her speeches, here or later (13:16a); only the pronoun *she* obtains. This subtle difference suggests the plight of the female. Without her name, she lacks power. Nonetheless, she speaks reason and wisdom.[36]

The words of Tamar fall on deaf ears. "He did not want to hear her voice" (13:14a). Passionately, Amnon has desired to see and touch her, for with these senses he has made of her what he wills. But to hear her voice is another matter; it disturbs the fantasies that eyes and hands have fashioned. To hear might mean repentance. So Amnon chooses to close out her voice, even leaving his refusal for the narrator to report. Amnon cares not at all for his sister. He acts against her will to pursue his lust.[37]

(d) Rape is the center of the chiasmus. Quickly, though with emphasis, the deed unfolds. Third-person narration distances the terror while reporting it. "He was stronger than she; thus he raped her and laid her" (13:14b). All three verbs come from the preceding section.[38] The one who "grabbed (*ḥzq*) hold of her" (13:11) is truly "stronger (*ḥzq*) than she." "Do not violate (*'nh*) me," she had pleaded (13:12); so "he raped (*'nh*) her." "Lie (*škb*) with me," he had ordered (13:11); now "he lay (*škb*)" not, however, with her because the Hebrew omits the preposition to stress his brutality. "He laid her."[39] If the repetitions of verbs confirm the predictability of Amnon's act, the direct object *her* underscores cruelty beyond the expected. The deed is done.

Violence in turn discloses hatred, the underside of lust. With profound insight, the storyteller interprets the terror of the act.

                a   b   c
Then-hated-her Amnon a-hatred great indeed (mě'ōd).

              c'   b'   a'
Truly (kî) great(er) the-hatred which he-hated-her
    than-the-desire which he-desired-her.

                                                (13:15ab)

Through a chiasmus of repeated words, the first two lines of this artfully constructed sentence focus hatred upon Tamar.[40] In the first line hate surrounds her (and Amnon too!), and in the second it attacks her through end-stress. Four times the verb and its cognate noun assault the victim. Structure and vocabulary secure hatred, and yet the sentence does not end. As a parallel in form to the second line, the third provides comparison and contrast. In using the word *desire* (*'hb*) to describe Amnon's feelings for Tamar (13:1, 4), this line shows that all along the desire was lust, not love. Having gratified itself, lust deepens into hatred. With all ambiguity eliminated, the two occurrences of the word *desire* yield to the four of *hate*.[41]

Then Amnon hated her a great hatred indeed.
Truly, greater was the hatred with which he hated her
    than the desire with which he desired her.
                                                (13:15ab)

Lust fulfilled escalates its attack on the victim. The crime is despicable; the aftermath, ominous.

c'-b'. A final conversation between Amnon and Tamar merges into command and response. Collapse of form and shrinkage of content show irreparable damage to the characters. Whereas preceding the crime four Hebrew words expressed Amnon's desire, "Come, lie with-me, my-sister" (13:11c), now two imperatives relay his revulsion, "Get-up; go" (13:15c). No longer does he call her sister or seek intimacy with her.[42] Instead, the imperative *go* (*hlk*) echoes derisively the command that first brought Tamar to his house, when David instructed her to go (*hlk*; 13:7).

This abused woman will no more heed Amnon's order of dismissal than she consented to his demand for rape. Nor does she allow anger to cloud her vision. If before the deed she sought justice, how much more after it! Though shorter this time, her words are equally firm.

They begin with the negative, "No (*'al*)." Unlike her earlier speech (13:12), the fraternal vocative is missing.[43] From Tamar's side, as from Amnon's, kinship language has ceased. "No," she said to him, "because sending me away is a greater evil than the other which you have done (*'śh*) to me" (13:16a).[44] If the narrator interprets that the hatred is greater than (*gĕdôlāh mē*) the desire, Tamar understands that the expulsion is greater than (*gĕdôlāh mē*) the rape. In sending her away, Amnon increases the violence he has inflicted upon her. He condemns her to a lifelong sentence of desolation (cf. 13:20b).

Tamar knows that rape dismissed is crime exacerbated. Yet she speaks to a foolish and hateful man who cares not at all for truth and justice, especially when embodied it stands in his presence. Before the crime, "he did not wish (*'bh*) to hear (*šmᶜ*) her voice" (13:14a); after the tragedy, he remains incorrigible. Hence comes the narrator's refrain, "But he was not willing (*'bh*) to listen (*šmᶜ*) to her" (13:16b). The words of this wise woman he spurns a second time.[45] She speaks no more.

a'. The conclusion of the chiasmus expands upon its opening.[46] Amnon orders "the young man attending him, 'Send out this from me to the outside and bolt the door after her'" (13:17). At the start, Amnon wanted the servants out and Tamar in (13:9de); at the close, he wants the servant in and Tamar out.[47] Although his two orders correspond, the Hebrew verbs differ. The imperative expelling Tamar (*šlḥ*) mocks her own words rather than reverting to Amnon's earlier vocabulary (*yṣ'*; 13:9de). "Sending (*šlḥ*) me away," she said, "is a greater evil than the other which you have done (*'śh*) to me." Amnon is capable of that evil. "Send (*šlḥ*) this away" (13:17b), he commands, speaking not to but about the woman who stands in his presence. She has become for him solely a disposable object. Furthermore, contrary to many translations,[48] he does not say, "Send away this woman from me." The Hebrew has only the demonstrative *this*. For Amnon, Tamar is a thing, a "this" he wants thrown out. She is trash. The one he desired before his eyes, his hatred wants outside, with the door bolted after her.

Yet his command receives delayed attention (cf. 13:9de). "Bolt the door after her" (*'aḥăreyāh*; 13:17c, RSV) leads to a narrative interlude beginning, "Now upon her" (*wĕᶜālêhā*; 13:18a). While

Amnon turns away from Tamar, the storyteller looks at her. Once again, she is the center of attention and once again without her name. "Now upon her was a long robe with sleeves, for thus were the virgin daughters of the king clad of old."[49] Sadly, what the robe proclaims Tamar is no longer. Filial and royal language has never attended this daughter of the king, and now the word *virgin* applies no more. Tamar is victim of a shame that her clothes cannot hide (cf. Gen. 2:25; 3:7).

Having placed the destroyed woman before our eyes, the narrator returns to the servant's response. At first glance, he appears to carry out the order precisely (cf. 13:9de). "He put her outside, the one attending him, and he bolted the door after her" (13:18b). Nuances show, however, that Amnon's power is waning. The description of Tamar has already broken the continuity between command and response. Moreover, when the servant does obey, Amnon ironically imprisons himself behind a locked door while releasing the proof of his crime. Further, though the imperative, "send out (*šlḥ*)," mocked Tamar's words (13:17), the storyteller halts the mocking. For the first time ever, narrated discourse fails to employ Amnon's vocabulary in reporting obedience to his command. Instead, the verb, "he put her outside" (*yṣ'*), matches the first occasion (13:9de) when the servants were sent out. These subtleties in the form and content imply that Amnon is a fool in Israel. Surely the responses to his last words recall Tamar's prediction (13:13a).

AFTER THE CRIME, 13:19-22

With the rape concluded, the plot moves to the aftermath: a meeting between Tamar and Absalom, a report on David, and a concluding description of characters and circumstances. These three episodes correspond, though with notable differences, to the three episodes before the crime. The first two units parallel in content and order the two immediately preceding the crime. The third episode returns to the opening verse of the story, thereby completing an overall ring composition (i.e., A, B, C, D, B', C', A').[50]

B'. *Tamar and Absalom, 13:19-20.* Before the crime a conversation between Jonadab and Amnon, centering upon Tamar, culminated in an appeal to David, the authority figure. Now, after the crime, a meeting between Tamar and Absalom, centering upon Amnon, matches this conversation. The meeting consists of narrated descriptions of Tamar (13:19 and 20c) encircling Absalom's words to her (13:20ab). The storyteller restores her name but removes her speech so that she continues to be powerless. In fact, she is the picture of desolation.

> Tamar took ashes upon her head
>   and the long robe that was upon her she tore.
> She put her hand upon her head,
>   and she went out; as she went, she wept.
>
> (13:19)[51]

Taking ashes upon her head employs the same verb (*lqḥ*) that marked Tamar's ministrations to Amnon: she took the dough, she took the pan, and she took the bread (13:8, 9, 10). Action intent upon restoring life to her sick brother becomes her own movement toward living death.[52] Further, tearing (*qrᶜ*) her long robe symbolizes the violence done to a virgin princess. Rape has torn (*ᶜnh*) her (13:14). The hand she puts upon her head is the hand from which Amnon feigned to eat as he grabbed hold of his sister (13:5, 6, 10, 11). A woman of mourning, Tamar goes away weeping.[53] Tears have replaced her voice of wisdom.

Through five separate occurrences, the verb describing her departure here, "she went away (*hlk*)," forms a circle for her actions in the story. The first word addressed to her, the word that altered her life forever, is the imperative, "Go." "And David sent to Tamar at the house, saying, 'Go (*hlk*) to the house of Amnon your brother'" (13:7). In the indicative, this verb characterizes her obedience: "Tamar went (*hlk*) to the house of Amnon her brother" (13:8). The central use of the verb, with a special meaning, belongs to Tamar. Trying to reason with Amnon, she asked, "And I, where would I carry (go with, *hlk*) my shame?" (13:13). The desolation implied in her question finds confirmation in the final appearances of the verb, which parallel the first two. Matching David's imperative is Amnon's last word to Tamar, "Go" (*hlk*; 13:15). To be sure, unlike the first occasion, she resists the order, but the outcome is inevitable. "She went away (*hlk*); as she went (*hlk*), she wept" (13:19d). For emphasis, the ending repeats the verb, joining it to her cry of pain. As this rhetorical circle closes, Tamar's actions cease.

Immediately Absalom speaks. His words form the center of the episode. While the presence of this prince has hovered over the story from the start (13:1), only now does he himself emerge. Continuing to stress kinship ties, the narrator introduces him as the brother of Tamar. Absalom appropriates the theme in addressing her.

> And Absalom her brother said to her,
> "Was Amnon your brother with you?
> Now, my sister, be quiet; your brother is he.
> Do not take to your heart this deed."
>
> (13:20ab)

Absalom's counsel surrounds his sister with the brother who has raped her, thereby repeating the circular structure that has ensnared Tamar from the beginning. Yet the narrator suggests a change. Standing over Amnon her brother is Absalom her brother. To him is the power of speech with layers of meaning. On the surface, his words appear to countenance the rape, only delicately alluded to at that. In the name of family loyalty, Absalom would silence Tamar, minimize the crime, and excuse Amnon.[54] But the interlocking structures and substance of the entire story indicate a different reading. In contrast to each of the other male characters, Absalom is the advocate of Tamar.

First, as advisor, he is to her what Jonadab was to Amnon. In urging Amnon to "act ill," Jonadab counseled pretense for a specific time and purpose. When he spoke of letting Tamar do the food so that Amnon could eat from her hand, his language cloaked a scheme for manipulation, seduction, and rape. With their own nuances, Absalom's advice to Tamar may also conceal a plan for revenge. "Be quiet . . . do not take to heart" counsels pretense for a time and purpose.[55] Absalom explicitly introduces this speech with the adverb *ʿattāh*, "now" or "for the time being" (cf. NJV). As Amnon's pretense deceived David, so Tamar's pretense will deceive Amnon. Further, rather than minimizing the crime, euphemisms such as "with you" or "this deed" underscore its horror. They cover the unspeakable, even as Jonadab's innocent vocabulary promoted rape. Clearly, Absalom counters Jonadab, though as advisor the brother cannot redeem for Tamar what she has lost.

Second, Absalom opposes Amnon. "Absalom her brother said to her, 'Was Amnon your brother with you?' . . . Your brother is he."

Fraternal language recalls the tension present in the opening verse
of the story where Absalom and Amnon surrounded Tamar (13:1).
Although Amnon seduced and polluted Tamar, Absalom supports
and protects her. In sentences that are grammatically parallel, both
brothers address her as "my sister," yet with different intents. For
Amnon, lust shapes the speech, "Come, lie with me, my sister"
(13:11). For Absalom, tenderness dictates the counsel, "For the
present, my sister, be quiet." Moreover, far from condoning Amnon's act, Absalom plots revenge.[56] Brother opposes brother
through their sister Tamar.

Third, Absalom counters David. By using David to overcome the
obstacle of Absalom, Jonadab and Amnon weakened the king's authority. Now Absalom speaks to Tamar on his own authority without
appeal to David. His position in the design of the story also indicates
that he supplants the king. If just before the crime David determined
the action, just after it Absalom takes charge. Speaking at the center
of this episode, he, not the king, orders the life of Tamar. Indeed,
as the only character to talk after the crime, he holds the power,
and this power he will use on behalf of Tamar. Thus, Absalom stands
apart from the other male characters, even though he cannot reverse
the desolation of his sister.

Like the beginning (13:19), the ending of this episode stresses the
ruin of Tamar. She lives in death.

> So Tamar dwelt, and she was desolate,
>   in the house of Absalom her brother.
>   (13:20c, RSV*)

In the first house (13:7a), she was a beautiful virgin (13:1, 2). In the
house of her brother Amnon (13:7b, 8), she became a violated thing
(13:14, 17). In the house of her brother Absalom (13:20c), she is a
desolate sister.[57] When used of people elsewhere in scripture, the
verb *be desolate* (*šmm*) connotes being destroyed by an enemy
(Lam. 1:16) or being torn to pieces by an animal (Lam. 3:11).[58]
Raped, despised, and rejected by a man, Tamar is a woman of sorrows and acquainted with grief. She is cut off from the land of the
living, stricken for the sins of her brother; yet she herself has done
no violence and there is no deceit in her mouth. No matter what
Absalom may plan for the future, the narrator understands the end-
less suffering of her present.

So Tamar dwelt, and she was desolate,
in the house of Absalom her brother.

In this description the storyteller continues to stress the fraternal bond. The repetition of the phrase, "Absalom her brother," matches the narrated introduction to his speech, "And Absalom her brother said to her" (13:20a). These words form a circle around the circle made by Absalom's use of the phrase "Amnon your brother" (13:20b). At the center of the two circles is Absalom's vocative, "my sister." It contrasts with Amnon's earlier use of the designation (13:11). If the brother Amnon has ensnared Tamar his sister, the brother Absalom surrounds them both to crush Amnon and comfort Tamar.[59] Form and content show that Absalom not only counters but overcomes Amnon.

C'. *David and His Children, 13:21.* Unlike the earlier conversation between Jonadab and Amnon, the meeting between Tamar and Absalom fails to culminate in an appeal to David. Even so, the second episode of the aftermath does turn to David through observations by the narrator. "When the king David heard all these deeds, he was very angry."[60] Inversion of the usual order of a Hebrew sentence, to place subject before verb, emphasizes the contrast between David and Absalom. Use of both title and name, "the king David," reinforces the dissimilarity. The royal rather than familial designation connotes power, yet power that forfeits responsibility. Though the brother Absalom has hinted at a plan, the king David has neither speech nor plan.

The received text says only that the king was "very angry." A Qumran manuscript adds, "for he loved him because his firstborn was he." The explanation suggests opposite interpretations. Is David angry at Amnon for what he has done, or is David angry about what has happened to Amnon? In other words, does the father's love for his firstborn condone or denounce the crime? The Greek Bible removes the ambiguity: "And he [David] did not rebuke Amnon his son because he loved him, since his firstborn was he."[61] David's anger signifies complete sympathy for Amnon and total disregard for Tamar. How appropriate that the story never refers to David and Tamar as father and daughter! The father identifies with the son; the adulterer supports the rapist; male has joined

male to deny justice for the female.[62] After all, in these days there
is a king in Israel, and royalty does the right in its own eyes.[63]
Truly, however, David the king does not do well to be angry
(cf. Jon. 4:4, 9).

A'. Conclusion: Characters and Circumstances, 13:22. With the
narrator still in charge, the last verse of the story returns to the first,
thereby completing the overall *inclusio*.

> Absalom did not speak (*dbr*) with Amnon
>   either evil or good,
> but Absalom hated Amnon on account of the deed (*dbr*)
>   that he raped Tamar his sister.
>
> (13:22)[64]

At the very beginning, Absalom and Amnon, identified as sons of
David, appeared in parallel positions surrounding Tamar. Tellingly,
Absalom's name came first, though the story moved with Amnon.

> To Absalom, son of David,
>   a sister beautiful, with the name Tamar,
> and desired her Amnon, son of David.
>
> (13:1)

Here, at the end (13:22), while David's name has appropriately dis-
appeared, the three central characters remain. No longer parallel,
the brothers meet as subject and object. Absalom does not speak
with Amnon, who has refused to hear the words of Tamar.[65] Absalom hates (*śn'*) Amnon, who hates (*śn'*) Tamar (13:15b). The fulfillment of Amnon's lust has replaced desire (*'hb*) with increasing
hatred, indeed a hatred turned upon Amnon himself.[66] His brother
Absalom, a greater obstacle than ever (cf. 13:4), holds the power.[67]
Foreboding silence cloaks fraternal hatred.

Tamar's position has also changed. No longer surrounded by two
brothers (cf. 13:20) nor desired by Amnon, she appears outside the
structure of their relationship. As in the opening verse of the story,
she is called the sister of Absalom, and yet this time no adjective
of beauty modifies the noun. Instead, a verb of violence acts upon
its object to defile; the sororal identification but underscores the
horror of the deed. The beautiful virgin encircled (13:1-2) has become the raped sister isolated (13:22). Her plight is the reason for

silence and hatred, and thus it is fitting that the end-stress of the story belongs to Tamar:

> but Absalom hated Amnon on account of the deed
> that he raped *Tamar his sister.*

RESPONSES TO THE CRIME

From Absalom and the Narrator. With its menace and foreboding silence, the conclusion of this story implies a sequel.[68] Absalom waits two years (13:23–39). Then, having persuaded his father to let Amnon visit at Baal Hazor,[69] Absalom orders him killed while Amnon was "merry with wine" (13:28, RSV). And it was done.[70] None other than the crafty Jonadab explains the murder to David: "For by the command of Absalom this has been determined from the day he [Amnon] raped (ʿnh) his sister Tamar" (13:32, RSV*).[71] Absalom flees. David mourns, though we cannot be sure if the object of his grief is Amnon the murdered or Absalom the fugitive.[72] We can be sure that it is not Tamar the violated.

After three years, Absalom returns to Jerusalem, but David refuses for a time to see him (14:1–33). Reporting these events, the narrator includes this description: "Now in all Israel there was no one so much to be praised for his beauty (*yph*) as Absalom; from the sole of his foot to the crown of his head there was no blemish in him" (14:25, RSV). *Beauty* is the same word once used for Tamar. Brother and sister were a handsome pair in Israel, but now the sister dwells desolate. The narrator has more to say on the subject, switching from Absalom to his offspring. "There were born to Absalom three sons and one daughter; her name was Tamar" (14:27, RSV*). Strikingly, the anonymity of all the sons highlights the name of the lone female child. In her Absalom has created a living memorial for his sister. A further note enhances the poignancy of his act. Tamar, the daughter of Absalom, "became a woman beautiful (*yph*) to behold." From aunt to niece have passed name and beauty so that rape and desolation have not the final word in the story of Tamar.

From the Readers. Absalom remembers; the narrator records; and we the readers respond.[73] If we cannot sanction the violent revenge Absalom exacted, we can appropriate the compassion he shows for his sister. Such appropriation leads to ironic reflections on a passage in Proverbs. As a textbook for young men,[74] Proverbs often exploits women for its own purposes. The foreign female symbolizes the wicked woman from whom Dame Wisdom[75] can protect the male.[76] Just such a contrast prevails when a teacher exhorts a young man:

> Say to wisdom, "My sister are you,"
>   and call insight an intimate friend
> to preserve you from the loose woman,
>   from the adventurer with her smooth words.
>   (Prov. 7:4–5, RSV*)

Only here does Proverbs designate wisdom as "sister."[77] The familial term resonates with our story because Amnon does call wisdom his sister.[78] Yet at this point ironies commence. "Come, lie with me, my sister," Amnon demanded, perverting the epithet to serve his lust. Tamar replied with wisdom:

> No, my brother.
> Do not violate me,
>   for it is not done thus in Israel.
> Do not do this foolish thing.
>   (13:12, RSV*)

Even after he raped her, she continued to speak wise words:

> No, because sending me away is a greater evil
>   than the other which you have done to me.
>   (13:16)

Obedient to the first line of the proverb, Amnon did say to Tamar the wise woman, "My sister are you." His embrace, however, produced a royal rape of wisdom. In light of his action, the parallel line heightens the contrast: "Call insight an intimate friend (or kinsman)." This advice Amnon skewed. For his intimate friend he chose the crafty Jonadab, who offered the plan that would gratify the lustful sight of the prince. Thus, iniquity, not insight, came from this kinsman.

Saying to wisdom, "My sister are you," and calling on an intimate friend for insight, Amnon was truly preserved "from the loose woman, from the adventurer with her smooth words." Yet *she* was never his temptation. His evil was his own lust, and from it others needed protection. Hence, Amnon's behavior exposes the misogynous assumption of this proverb to inspire a different perspective. Moreover, compassion for Tamar requires a new vision. If sister wisdom can protect a young man from the loose woman, who will protect sister wisdom from the loose man, symbolized not by a foreigner but by her very own brother? Who will preserve sister wisdom from the adventurer, the rapist with his smooth words, lecherous eyes, and grasping hands? In answering the question, Israel is found wanting—*and so are we.*

NOTES

1. With perhaps a few additional passages, 2 Samuel 9—20 and 1 Kings 1—2 constitute the larger narrative. On the historical issues, see, most recently, John Van Seters, *In Search of History* (New Haven and London: Yale University Press, 1983), pp. 277–91. For bibliographies through 1978, see D. M. Gunn, *The Story of King David*, JSOT Supp. 6 (Sheffield: JSOT Press, 1978), pp. 142–53; Charles Conroy, *Absalom Absalom! Narrative and Language in 2 Sam 13–20* (Rome: Biblical Institute Press, 1978), pp. 155–73. Within this larger narrative, Conroy establishes 2 Samuel 13—20 as an originally independent unit (pp. 1–6, 86–114), a view accepted by P. Kyle McCarter, Jr., "'Plots, True or False': The Succession Narrative as Court Apologetic," *Int* 35 (1981): 362–63; cf. Peter R. Ackroyd, who designates 2 Samuel 13—19 as the unit in "The Succession Narrative (so-called)," *Int* 35 (1981): 385–86. R. A. Carlson isolates 2 Samuel 13—14 as a unit; see *David, the Chosen King: A Traditio-Historical Approach to the Second Book of Samuel* (Stockholm: Almqvist & Wiksell, 1964), pp. 163–67. To this section belongs our story, which is itself a unit.
2. Recent literary studies include George Ridout, "The Rape of Tamar: A Rhetorical Analysis of 2 Sam 13:1–22," in *Rhetorical Criticism*, ed. Jared J. Jackson and Martin Kessler (Pittsburgh: Pickwick Press, 1974), pp. 75–84; Conroy, *Absalom Absalom!* pp. 17–39; J. P. Fokkelman, *King David*, vol. 1, *Narrative Art and Poetry in the Books of Samuel* (Assen, The Netherlands: Van Gorcum, 1981), pp. 99–114. Kiyoshi K. Sacon, "A Study of the Literary Structure of 'The Succession Narrative,'" in *Studies in the Period of David and Solomon and Other Essays*, ed. Tomoo Ishida (Winona Lake, Ind.: Eisenbrauns, 1982), pp. 27–54. Available to me only in a brief English abstract is the work of S. Bar-Efrat, *Literary Modes and Methods in the Biblical Narrative, in view of II Sam. 10—20; I Kings 1—2* (in Hebrew); but see his article, "Some Observations on the Analysis of Structure in Biblical Narrative," *VT* 30 (1980): especially 162–63. In contrast, not opposition, to these studies, I employ a feminist perspective so that hermeneutical emphases differ even when literary observations concur.
3. Wherever they are not identified in this essay, chapter and verse citations come from the book of 2 Samuel.
4. By including 13:4 in this first episode, Ridout misses the ring structure

and also breaks the direct discourse of 13:4-5; see "The Rape of Tamar," p. 81.

5. Though none of the three children has appeared before, the names of the sons occur in the family chronicle (2 Sam. 3:2-3). On the matrilinear rivalry of Amnon and Absalom, see Jon D. Levenson and Baruch Halpern, "The Political Import of David's Marriages," *JBL* 99 (1980): 507-18. The daughter Tamar is truly a new character. Half sister of one brother and full sister of the other, she lacks a place in the list of David's offspring. The omission resonates with our story. While the language of father and son persists, the language of father and daughter never occurs.

6. Contrary to translations that identify Amnon's yearning (*'hb*) as love (e.g., RSV, NEB, and NAB), I have chosen the ambiguous word *desire* to let the plot disclose the precise meaning (cf. NJV).

7. On the importance of relational epithets, see Ridout, "The Rape of Tamar," pp. 75-78; also Robert Alter, *The Art of Biblical Narrative* (New York: Basic Books, 1981), p. 180.

8. For negative meanings of the phrase, "to do . . . anything," see Gen. 22:12 and Jer. 39:12.

9. On the morally neutral quality of "crafty" (*ḥkm*), see R. N. Whybray, *The Succession Narrative* (Naperville, Ill.: Alec R. Allenson, 1968), p. 58; idem, *The Intellectual Tradition in the Old Testament* (Berlin: Walter de Gruyter, 1974), pp. 89-93.

10. *Contra* Conroy, *Absalom Absalom!* p. 28, Jonadab's question is not necessarily "an admission of ignorance," perhaps already "insinuating a pejorative judgment on the quality of this shrewdness." As a skilled counselor, Jonadab observes Amnon's condition and then invites the prince to discuss his problem.

11. These are all connotations of the adjective *dal*.

12. See Harry Hagan, "Deception as Motif and Theme in 2 Sm 9—20; 1 Kgs 1—2," *Biblica* 60 (1979): 308-10.

13. Note the chiastic arrangement of the sequence feeding/preparing// seeing/eating.

14. *Contra* Burke O. Long, "Wounded Beginnings: David and Two Sons," in *Images of Man and God*, ed. Burke O. Long (Sheffield: Almond Press, 1981), pp. 28, 116 n. 20. The verb *see* (*r'h*) also plays on the perspective that Jonadab gives Amnon as well as on the forthcoming visit of David to see (*r'h*) this sick man (13:6).

15. For further evaluation of Jonadab, see Fokkelman, *King David*, p. 109.

16. A comparison of Jonadab's words (13:5b) with Amnon's version (13:6b) discloses the following: (a) The opening lines are identical. (b) Jonadab uses the neutral words *lḥm* and *bryh* for bread and food, while Amnon switches to a special term (*lbbt*) suggesting an erotic pun (see below). (c) The phrase "before my eyes" appears in both speeches to play upon the narrator's statement that "it seemed impossible in the eyes of Amnon to do to her anything" (13:2). (d) Though Jonadab proposed two petitions, feeding and preparing the food, Amnon cites one, the making of bread. (e) Similarly, Amnon modifies the results desired. While Jonadab spoke of seeing and eating (*'kl*) "from her hand," Amnon omits the seeing, uses a

different verb for eating (*brh*), but retains the phrase "from her hand." Such stylistic variations delineate the characters.

17. See Conroy, *Absalom Absalom!* p. 29f, especially note 43; Fokkelman, *King David*, pp. 105–6; cf. Hans Wilhelm Hertzberg, *I & II Samuel*, OTL (Philadelphia: Westminster Press, 1964), p. 323.

18. Two of Amnon's telling phrases David omits: "before my [his] eyes"; "that I [he] may eat from her [your] hand." Further, though Amnon has requested the bread (*lbbt*) his heart desires, the bread (*bryh*) David orders reverts to the vocabulary of Jonadab. Hence, David avoids these dangerous words but retains the ominous verb *make* or *do* ('*śh*) that the narrator introduced (13:2), Jonadab appropriated (13:5b), and Amnon embraced (13:6b).

19. On the importance of command and response, see Conroy, *Absalom Absalom!* pp. 19, 37–38.

20. Note that the narrator views the occasion through the eyes of Amnon to designate the bread as special food (*lbbt*), the desire of his heart, rather than as the standard nourishment that Jonadab and David have specified.

21. See Long, "Wounded Beginnings," p. 28.

22. This central unit is the D section in the overall composition; see the schema given in the second paragraph of this chapter.

23. Though parallel in form, these sections diverge in length and content. Longer than the beginning (13:9de), the ending (13:17–19) contains a parenthetical note from the narrator (13:18a) that separates direct command and response.

24. Note that the structural collapse follows the rape. Thus defects in structure mark the injury to the characters themselves; rape violates the orderly patterns of life.

25. While the surrounding sections mix direct and narrated discourse, only the latter reports the rape, thereby distancing it.

26. See the comments on 13:1–3 above.

27. On the narrator's role in the story, see Conroy, *Absalom Absalom!* pp. 22–26; cf. Whybray, *The Succession Narrative*, pp. 15–16. On the omniscience and inobtrusiveness of the biblical narrator, see Alter, *The Art of Biblical Narrative*, pp. 183–85.

28. Shrewdly, Amnon switches to the neutral word for food (*bryh* instead of *lbbt*) as he speaks to the woman his appetite craves.

29. The epithet "her brother" underscores the familial theme that permeates the story.

30. On *ḥzq*, cf. Judg. 19:25, 29. See chapter 3, below.

31. In Hebrew each of these four short words ends with the same vowel sound (*î*) to yield emphatic assonance (cf. 13:4). They also play with earlier vocabulary. "Come (*bô'î*)": As much as any other, this word (*bô'*) has moved the story to its center. Following the plans of Jonadab, David came to Amnon to hear the request, "Let Tamar my sister come" (13:5, 6). "Lie (*šikbî*)": Used three times to describe the position of Amnon (13:5, 6, 8), this verb (*škb*) assumes now a different meaning. The sick son lying down is the lustful brother seeking to lie with his sister. "Lie with me ('*immî*)": The pronoun *me* recalls the emphasis with which Amnon confessed his selfish longings to Jonadab. "I ('*ănî*)," he stressed, "desire" (13:4).

"Come, lie with me, my sister (*'ăḥôtî*)": The vocative calls forth conflicting associations. In the love poetry of Israel, "my sister" is an address of respect and endearment (cf. SS 4:9, 10, 12; 5:1-2), but on the lips of Amnon it is betrayal and seduction (cf. 13:5, 6). Appetite parades as affection; entrapment as endearment.

32. On the technique of contrastive dialogue, see Alter, *The Art of Biblical Narrative*, pp. 72-74. Unlike Alter, I do not see Tamar's lengthy speech as a "kind of panicked catalogue."

33. Conroy finds here a concentric sentence structure; see *Absalom Absalom!* p. 31:

A   Emphatic prohibition: No, my brother; do not violate me.

B   Reason clause: for it is not done thus in Israel.

A' Restatement of the prohibition: Do not do this foolish thing.

34. On meanings of the term *nĕbālāh* (foolish thing), see Anthony Phillips, "*Nebalah*—a term for serious disorderly and unruly conduct," *VT* 25 (1975): 237-41. For sexual references, cf. Gen. 34:7; Deut. 22:21; Judg. 19:23-24. For this word and others, Carlson notes an associative basis in Judges 19—21; see Carlson's *David, the Chosen King*, pp. 165-67; also see chapter 3 below.

35. On the legality of a marriage between Tamar and Amnon, see Conroy, *Absalom Absalom!* pp. 17-18, notes 3 and 4; also Phillips, "*Nebalah*," p. 239.

36. Hagan calls her "the real wise one in the story"; see "Deception as Motif and Theme," p. 310.

37. Rape, not incest, is Amnon's crime; see Conroy, *Absalom Absalom!* p. 18 n. 4; Fokkelman, *King David*, pp. 103-4. *Contra* James W. Flanagan, "Court History or Succession Document? A Study of 2 Samuel 9—20 and 1 Kings 1—2," *JBL* 91 (1972): 180; and, apparently, Long, "Wounded Beginnings," p. 27. My use of the phrase "against her will" comes from Susan Brownmiller's study of rape: *Against Our Will* (New York: Simon & Schuster, 1975), p. 18.

38. On the three levels of violence, see Fokkelman, *King David*, pp. 106-7.

39. On the pilgrimage of the verb *škb*, see ibid., pp. 104-5.

40. See Ridout, "The Rape of Tamar," p. 83. Fokkelman's pairing of *mĕ'ōd* and *kî* is not altogether convincing (*King David*, p. 107). Though these two words fit the concentric structure, they, unlike the other pairs, are not repetitions.

41. Thus far, *desire* and *hate* are evenly matched with four appearances each (13:1, 4, 15). But the imbalance in the center of the story (13:15) shows hatred overtaking the ambiguity of desire; in the end, it will surpass (see 13:22).

42. *Contra* Fokkelman, *King David*, p. 108, the halves of this chiasmus of command do not "precisely match up with each other." The point is that rape has destroyed the perfect symmetry of form, content, and characters.

43. Though the Hebrew text of 13:16 is unclear, the fraternal vocative is not there (see ASV, NEB, NJV). Those translations in which "my

brother" appears follow the Lucian recension of the Greek Bible (e.g., RSV, JB, and NAB; see S. R. Driver, *Notes on the Hebrew Text and the Topography of the Books of Samuel* [Oxford: At the Clarendon Press, 1960], pp. 298–99). Ridout observes that the Lucian reading provides an exact parallel to the vocative in 13:12, thereby enhancing the overall symmetry of 13:11–14a and 13:15b–16; see "The Rape of Tamar," pp. 82–83. Fokkelman agrees; see *King David*, p. 108. But the omission of the vocative in Hebrew fits well the flawed symmetry that characterizes the entire unit. Again, rape disturbs form and content as it alters the characters.

44. Note the absence of Tamar's name in the introduction to her words. "But she said to him" (13:16) contrasts with, "And Amnon said to her" (13:15c). See the comments above on 13:12–13.

45. In calling Tamar a wise woman (*'iššâ ḥăkāmâ*), I employ terminology that is not in the text. Yet the designation fits. Speaking with the authority of custom, Tamar reasons and counsels with Amnon. Her use of the word *fool* (*nbl*) is characteristic of sapiential speech (13:12–13). Cf. Claudia V. Camp, "The Wise Women of 2 Samuel: A Role Model for Women in Early Israel?" *CBQ* 43 (1981): 14–29.

46. Perhaps this expansion compensates in length for the missing segment in the flawed chiasmus, where c' and b' merge (13:15c–16). Note that the alternative structure proposed by Ridout separates the command of 13:17 from its response in 13:18b. Further, by making 13:18–19 a unit, this proposed structure mixes action within Amnon's house (13:18) with action outside (13:19) and also fails to see the unit present in 13:19–20. See "The Rape of Tamar," p. 81.

47. Fokkelman observes that "the servants and Tamar form a chiastic pattern of motion [13:8–9 and 13:17–18] about the centre, the horrible tête-à-tête of Amnon and Tamar in vv. 10–16"; see *King David*, p. 102.

48. E.g., ASV, RSV, NEB, and NJV; cf. NAB.

49. Only here does the word *daughter* (*bat*) appear in the story. Note that the use is generic, not specific. On the textual problem in this verse (Hebrew *mě'îlîm*), see Driver, *Notes on the Hebrew Text*, pp. 299–300; Gunn, *The Story of King David*, pp. 32–33.

50. Structurally, the unit combines chiasmus and alternation; see H. Van Dyke Parunak, "Oral Typesetting: Some Uses of Biblical Structure," *Biblica* 62 (1981): 153–68.

51. On the artistry of this sentence, see Fokkelman, *King David*, pp. 109–10.

52. See Conroy, *Absalom Absalom!* p. 34.

53. Cf. Esther 4:1 and 2 Kings 5:8.

54. Conroy fails to acknowledge these possibilities. Too easily he describes Absalom's words as "consolation," embracing a "gentle command" and a "mild prohibition" to "convey a tone of tenderness." See *Absalom Absalom!* pp. 34–35.

55. Elsewhere in scripture the imperative, "be quiet" (*ḥrš*, Hiphil), is a warning (Judg. 18:19), sometimes that the speaker wishes to be heard (Job 13:13; Isa. 41:1). Fokkelman interprets this command juridically: "Don't involve yourself actively in this matter." See *King David*, pp. 110–11. Similarly, cf. J. Hoftijzer, "Absalom and Tamar: A Case of Fratriarchy?" in

Schrift en uitleg: W. H. Gispen Festschrift, ed. Dirk Attema et al. (Kampen: J. H. Kok, 1970), p. 60, note 18.

56. As Amnon's power wanes behind the bolted door, Absalom's rises on the public scene. See the aftermath of this story, leading to Absalom's challenge to David for the throne (13:23—15:18).

57. The repetitions of the phrase, "house (*byt*) of . . . brother (*'ḥ*)" in 13:7, 8, and 20b accent further the fraternal contrast. On the concentric structure of space ringed by the word *house*, see Fokkelman, *King David*, pp. 102–3.

58. See also Isa. 54:1. The verb *šmm* is often applied to land that is plundered, raped, and destroyed (e.g., Isa. 49:8; Ezek. 33:28). Utterly inadequate to convey the meaning here is the translation "sad and lonely" (2 Sam. 13:20c in the *Good News Bible*).

59. See Fokkelman, *King David*, pp. 111–12, who follows Bar-Efrat. Cf. also the circular compositions of 13:1, 2, 15a.

60. By a skillful use of vocabulary, the opening clause of this sentence connects the monarch to each of his sons: "When the king David heard all these deeds. . . ." The verb *hear* (*šmʿ*) recalls Amnon's refusal to hear Tamar (13:14, 16), and the object *deeds* (*dbr*) employs Absalom's own allusion to the rape (13:20). In the father the sons compete. Yet the episode in its entirety resolves the tension to contrast David with Absalom and identify him with Amnon.

61. See McCarter, "'Plots, True or False,'" p. 366, especially note 20.

62. Amnon's rape of Tamar recalls David's adultery with Bathsheba (2 Samuel 11); father and son are enmeshed in sensual sin. For a comparison of these events, see Gunn, *The Story of King David*, pp. 98–100; see also Kenneth R. R. Gros Louis, "The Difficulty of Ruling Well: King David of Israel," in *Semeia* 8, ed. Robert W. Funk (Missoula, Mont.: Scholars Press, 1977), p. 30.

63. Cf. the rapes of the concubine and others "in those days when there was no king in Israel" (Judges 19—21); see chapter 3 below.

64. Fokkelman shows the concentric arrangement formed in Hebrew by the root *dbr* enclosing the two occurrences of the pair Absalom/Amnon as subject and object; see *King David*, p. 112. Through exclusion, this arrangement highlights the rape of Tamar; it receives the end-stress of the sentence. On end-stress, see Axel Olrik, "Epic Laws of Folk Narrative," in *The Study of Folklore*, ed. Alan Dundas (Englewood Cliffs, N.J.: Prentice-Hall, 1965), pp. 136–37. On the translation, "but (*kî*) Absalom hated Amnon . . ." see Hoftijzer, "Absalom and Tamar: A Case of Fratriarchy?" pp. 55–56.

65. On the importance of a narrator's explicit notice of silence, see Alter, *The Art of Biblical Narrative*, p. 79. Other interpretations of the phrase "did not speak . . . evil or good" include (a) the failure to take legal action (W. Malcolm Clark, "A Legal Background to the Yahwist's Use of 'Good and Evil' in Genesis 2—3," *JBL* 88 [1969]: 269); (b) the lack of hostile treatment (Fokkelman, *King David*, p. 112).

66. Before the crime, *desire* occurs twice (13:1, 4). At the crime, *desire* again occurs twice, here in parallelism to *hatred*; the word *hatred* itself appears four times (13:15a). In all these instances, Amnon is the subject of

the verbs and Tamar the object. Moreover, the two words *desire* and *hatred* appear the same number of times. After the crime, however, *desire* disappears, but *hatred* continues, with Absalom as its subject and Amnon its object (13:22). Altogether, hatred (five occurrences) surpasses desire (four occurrences). Lust fulfilled increases into hatred.

67. As commentators note (e.g., Hertzberg, *I & II Samuel*, p. 326), Absalom may also be motivated by a desire for the throne. This interpretation, however, is extrinsic to the story; see Conroy, *Absalom Absalom!* p. 36, note 75.

68. On thematic connections between the story and its surroundings, see Hertzberg, *I & II Samuel*, pp. 322, 326–28; Whybray, *The Succession Narrative*, p. 22; Long, "Wounded Beginnings," pp. 27, 30–34. On literary connections, see Gunn, *The Story of King David*, pp. 98–100; Flanagan, "Court History or Succession Document?" p. 180; Gros Louis, "The Difficulty of Ruling Well," pp. 15–33; Fokkelman, *King David*, pp. 101, 114–25. On Absalom's story, see Zvi Adar, *The Biblical Narrative* (Jerusalem: Department of Education and Culture of the World Zionist Organisation, 1959), pp. 142–97; Jacob Licht, *Storytelling in the Bible* (Jerusalem: Magnes Press, 1978), pp. 12–13; 41–48.

69. See Hagan, "Deception as Motif and Theme," pp. 310–11.

70. In having Amnon murdered, Absalom reflects David who had Uriah murdered (2 Sam. 11:6–21). The father lives in the son.

71. See Hoftijzer, "Absalom and Tamar: A Case of Fratriarchy?" pp. 55–61.

72. Though the reference to David's mourning "for his son" might appropriately refer to Amnon, who has just been murdered, the immediate antecedent (13:37) is Absalom.

73. A modern novel based on this story is Dan Jacobson, *The Rape of Tamar* (Middlesex, England: Penguin Books, 1973).

74. See Whybray, *The Succession Narrative*, pp. 65–66; cf. James L. Crenshaw, *Old Testament Wisdom* (Atlanta: John Knox Press, 1981), pp. 27–36.

75. To choose a title for the female personification of wisdom is difficult. Such designations as "Lady Wisdom" and "Dame Wisdom" do convey the elitism that marks this figure in Proverbs. From a feminist perspective, the portrayal is ambivalent. Although these texts seemingly honor woman, wisdom is woman on a pedestal who is used to attract men.

76. See William McKane, *Proverbs* (Philadelphia: Westminster Press, 1970), pp. 284–87 and *passim*; Crenshaw, *Old Testament Wisdom*, pp. 96–99.

77. See McKane, *Proverbs*, p. 334.

78. In using this verse from Proverbs, I am not proposing any intentional links between it and our story in the manner, e.g., of Whybray, *The Succession Narrative*, pp. 71–75, 78–95. Cf. J. L. Crenshaw, "Method in Determining Wisdom Influence upon 'Historical' Literature," *JBL* 88 (1969): 137–40.

AN
UNNAMED
WOMAN

Concubine
from Bethlehem

Her body was broken
and given to many.

CHAPTER 3

An Unnamed Woman
The Extravagance of Violence

Judges 19:1–30

The betrayal, rape, torture, murder, and dismemberment of an unnamed woman is a story we want to forget but are commanded to speak. It depicts the horrors of male power, brutality, and triumphalism; of female helplessness, abuse, and annihilation. To hear this story is to inhabit a world of unrelenting terror that refuses to let us pass by on the other side.

Belonging to the close of the book of Judges,[1] the story reflects a time when leaders were lacking, God seldom appeared, and chaos reigned among the Israelite tribes. Repeatedly, the Deuteronomic editor characterizes this period with the indictment, "In those days there was no king in Israel."[2] What is not accounts for what is: that "every man ('*îš*) did what was right in his own eyes."[3] Such internal anarchy produces violence and vengeance, as the narratives about the tribe of Benjamin amply demonstrate (chapters 19—21).[4]

Of the three acts that organize these Benjaminite traditions,[5] the first claims our attention.[6] In design, an introduction (19:1–2) and a conclusion (19:29–30) surround two scenes (19:3–10 and 19:15b–28), while an interlude separates them (19:11–15a). With Israel as the larger setting, the geographical movement of the act is circular, beginning and ending in the hill country of Ephraim. Bethlehem in Judah is the location of scene one and Gibeah in Benjamin of scene two. The interlude, focused on Jebus, bridges the distance between them. In content, the two scenes are studies in hospitality. The first portrays a familial gathering and the second a communal reception. Frequent use of the word *house* or *home* (*byt*) underscores their common subject matter. By contrast, the word does not appear in the interlude, for Jebus is a foreign city.

The cast of characters is predominantly male: a Levite, his attendant (*n'r*),[7] a father, an old man, and a group of men. Of the two females, a concubine is central; a virgin daughter receives scant attention. All these people are nameless. The men do speak, even the attendant, but the women say nothing. Though most of the characters appear only in sections of the act, each contributes to the overriding theme of turbulent life moving circuitously to violent death. The path is tortuous and torturous. Our task is to make the journey alongside the concubine: to be her companion in a literary and hermeneutical enterprise.

DESERTION

Introduction: Judges 19:1–2

At the beginning, the narrator introduces the two main characters through polarities of sex, status, and geography. "A man, a Levite sojourning in the remote hill country of Ephraim" opposes "a woman, a concubine from Bethlehem of Judah" (19:1). Structurally, these descriptions correspond. Man ('*îš*) and woman ('*iššâ*) are parallel identifications. The remote and unspecified hill country of Ephraim in the north balances the accessible and familiar town of Bethlehem in the south. Similarly, the middle terms, Levite and concubine, match. Yet their meaning poses striking dissonance. A Levite has an honored place in society that sets him above many other males;[8] a concubine has an inferior status that places her beneath other females. Legally and socially, she is not the equivalent of a wife but is virtually a slave, secured by a man for his own purposes.[9] The grammar and syntax of this opening sentence exploit the inequality. "A man, a Levite sojourning in the remote hill country of Ephraim took for himself a woman, a concubine from Bethlehem of Judah." He is subject; she, object. He controls her. How he acquired her we do not know; that he owns her is certain.

What a surprise it is, then, to read the next sentence in which subject and object reverse. The lowly concubine acts (19:2). Perhaps her unexpected initiative accounts for the confusion about her conduct. Two manuscript traditions have survived.[10] The Hebrew (MT) and Syriac claim that "his concubine played the harlot" against the Levite, while the Greek and Old Latin maintain that "his concubine became angry with him." At issue is the identity of the offended party. Was she unfaithful to him or did he cause her anger? Ancient manuscripts give contradictory answers; the story itself allows either reading. All versions agree, however, upon the second action of the concubine: she left the Levite for "her father's house at Bethlehem in Judah and was there some four months" (19:2; cf. 19:3b). Returning to her native land, the woman increases the distance between herself and her master.[11] Though called his concubine, she deserts him.[12] Her action in going home introduces a third character to set up another polarity. Father opposes master, with the daughter/concubine in the middle. Resolution of the tensions awaits scene one.

PURSUIT AND NEGLECT

Scene One: Judges 19:3–10

This scene comprises three episodes: the journey of the master to Bethlehem (19:3abc), the visit in the father's house (19:3d–9), and the departure (19:10).[13]

A. *Episode One, 19:3abc.* Just as "she went (*hlk*) from him" (19:2), so now "he went (*hlk*) after her" (19:3). But his pursuit fails to resolve the ambiguity of her desertion. He went after her, says the Hebrew, "to speak to her heart (*lēb*), to bring her back."[14] The words, "to speak to the heart," connote reassurance, comfort, loyalty, and love. In other passages where this phrase describes the action of a man toward a woman, she may be either the offended or the guilty party. For example, after raping Dinah, the daughter of Lean and Jacob, Shechem found himself drawn to her; "he loved the young woman and spoke to her heart" (Gen. 34:3). Yet in the prophecy of Hosea, Yahweh, the faithful lover, promises to restore his faithless bride Israel, to bring her into the wilderness and to "speak to her heart" (Hos. 2:14[16]). Thus, the Levite's speaking to the heart of his concubine indicates love for her without specifying guilt. The narrative censures no one for the concubine's departure. Moreover, it portrays the master sympathetically. Be the woman innocent or guilty, he seeks reconciliation. Accompanied by his attendant and a couple of donkeys, he journeys to "her father's house" (19:3b). The phrase, "to her father's house," at the end of this unit matches the same phrase at the close of the introduction (19:2). Such vocabulary is telling because the hospitality of the father-in-law, rather than a meeting between the Levite and his concubine, governs episode two.

B. *Episode Two, 19:3d–9.* Time periods of shrinking length mark the visit of the master to Bethlehem: three days, another day and night, and a final day. In each of them the father-in-law dominates, though with diminishing power. When he ceases to prevail, the visit ends. Strikingly, as the three periods decrease, the accounts of them increase so that the closer the departure, the longer the delay.[15] The narrated expansion corresponds to the buildup of tension. This pattern foreshadows scene two, the heart of terror, in which the shortest period of time yields the longest narrative and the greatest tension.

The father greets the master with joy. As these two unite, the woman who brought them together fades from the scene. Truly, this version of oriental hospitality is an exercise in male bonding.

> And his father-in-law, the father of the young woman,
>   made him stay;[16]
> and he remained with him three days;
> so they ate and drank and spent the night.[17]
>
> On the fourth day *they* got up early in the morning,
>   and *he* arose to go.
>
> (19:4–5a)

The switch from a plural to a singular pronoun, from *they* to *he*, shows that the woman is not counted in either verb. The two men got up, and one prepared to leave. At this point, direct discourse empowers the father's wish. To the master who came to speak to the heart of his concubine (19:3a), her father says, "Strengthen your heart with a morsel of bread and after that you may go" (19:5b, RSV).[18] The plural form of the verb, "you may go," contrasts with the singular imperative, "strengthen." If this plural includes the woman, along with the attendant and the donkeys, the succeeding action explicitly omits her. "So the two men sat and ate and drank together" (19:6, RSV). Neither food nor drink nor companionship attends the female, but the males enjoy it all. Further, having weakened the resolve of the master through generous hospitality, the father of the young woman seeks again to detain him. "Please stay and let your heart enjoy" (19:6). Though he meets resistance, the father-in-law succeeds; the master "sat and spent the night" (19:7). Hence, the fourth day ends as did the first three (19:4).

For the final period of the visit, two speeches from the father, of increasing length, supplement narrated discourse (19:8–9). While similarities with the earlier periods remain, important differences emerge. Unlike their action the preceding day, the two men do not rise up together. "And he [the master] got up early in the morning of the fifth day to go" (19:8a). Unity between the males begins to dissolve. Nevertheless, the father-in-law detains his guest. "Strengthen now your heart," he implores (19:8b). His request begins an argument that lasts most of the day (19:8c).[19] At the end, the two of them eat together (19:8d), once again excluding the woman (cf. 19:6).

Immediately afterward the master arises to go—not only he but also his concubine and attendant (19:9a). For the narrator to specify concubine and attendant indicates the resoluteness of the master's intention, and yet the father tries one final time (19:9). Twice he uses the Hebrew word hinnēh, usually translated behold, to emphasize his message.[20] He observes the danger of travel at night; he cites his hospitality as incentive to stay;[21] and he promises an early departure the next day. "Tomorrow," he says, "you shall arise early in the morning for your journey and go to your tent" (19:9e). Surely, the reference to the tent suggests an unfavorable comparison to "the father's house" (19:2, 3b) with its lavish entertainment. Rivalry between the males has replaced unity. But the many words of the father are not persuasive. The more he talks, the less he achieves. By contrast, the master, who has said nothing, emerges the victor.[22]

The power struggle between the two men highlights the plight of the woman who brought them together but whom they and the storyteller have ignored. Unlike her father, the daughter has no speech; unlike her master, the concubine has no power. A journey "to speak to her heart" has become a visit to engage male hearts, with no speech to her at all. What the master set out to do, he has forsaken to enjoy hospitality and competition with another man. The woman suffers through neglect.[23]

C. *Episode Three, 19:10.* Juxtaposed to the first episode, the third matches it in brevity but contrasts with it in content. As the master earlier journeyed to Bethlehem, so now he leaves. Eager to depart, he risks the dangers of travel toward evening. Quickly the storyteller sets distance by bringing him "opposite Jebus (that is, Jerusalem)."[24] With him were "a couple of donkeys and his concubine and his attendant." Having first arrived in Bethlehem with two possessions, his attendant and a couple of donkeys (19:3b), the master appears at Jebus with three, the woman having been put in this category. Thus concludes scene one.

AN INTERLUDE OF CONTINUING NEGLECT

Judges 19:11–15a

Since the return trip begins late, the travelers cannot complete the journey to Ephraim in a single day. Hence, the narrative provides an interlude for decision making. It begins near Jebus (19:11a) and ends at Gibeah (19:14–15a). A conversation between the attendant and his master covers the distance (19:11b–13).[25]

The attendant proposes that the group spend the night in Jebus (19:11), but the master, speaking for the first time, refuses because it is a "city of foreigners who do not belong to the people of Israel" (19:13, RSV). He chooses to press on to Gibeah, or perhaps Ramah.[26] Though his reasoning makes sense, he knows not the violent irony of his decision. In their exchange, two males again ignore the female. They do not ask her preference for the night. If the attendant is subordinate to the master, she is inferior to them both. Her sex as female, not her status as servant, makes her powerless. Like the donkeys, she belongs only in the "they" who turn aside "to go in and spend the night at Gibeah." The stage is set for scene two.

THE ATTENTION OF VIOLENCE

Scene Two: Judges 19:15b–28

In the earlier report of the master's visit to the house of his father-in-law, narrative length increased as tension mounted. Such coordination of length and conflict foreshadowed the development of scene two. The time of this scene is a single night in Gibeah, and yet the length exceeds significantly the entire account of five days in Bethlehem. The cast of characters enlarges, though the master still dominates. Like the opening scene, this one is a study in oriental hospitality. It becomes, however, a saga of violence.[27] Two episodes organize the action. The first moves from the public square to a house in Gibeah (19:15b–21); the second from the house to the outside and back again (19:22–28).

A. *Episode One, 19:15b–21.* In this episode narrated discourse (19:15b–17a and 19:21) surrounds a conversation between males (19:17b–20). In turn, the dialogue repeats the pattern: two speeches by the old man (19:17b and 19:20) surround the words of the master (19:18–19). Crucial to the symmetry of the unit is the word *house* (*byt*). It appears once at the beginning (19:15b), once at the end (19:21), and twice in the middle (19:18).[28] Hospitality is emphatically the issue.

The master enters the city of Gibeah.[29]

> And he went in and sat in the open square of the city;
> no man took them into his house to spend the night.
> (19:15b, RSV*)

Having rejected Jerusalem because it is a "city of foreigners," the master finds no reception among the people of Gibeah. The tribal town becomes the alien place. Moreover, the introduction of another character, who resides here temporarily, heightens the irony.[30]

> Now (*hinnēh*) an old man was coming
>   from his work in the field at evening;
> the man was from the hill country of Ephraim,
>   and he was sojourning in Gibeah.
> The men of the place were Benjaminites.
> (19:16, RSV)

A sojourner in Benjamin, in fact, one from the territory of the master, will provide the hospitality that the natives do not offer—only to demonstrate its severe limitations.

Lifting up his eyes, the old man sees the wayfarer in the open square of the city. "Where are you going (*hlk*) and from where have you come (*bô'*)?" he asks (19:17, RSV*).[31] Destiny and origin, rather than present situation, are his questions, but the master's reply intertwines all three concerns (19:18). First, acknowledging his traveling companions, he describes the present situation:

> We are passing over from Bethlehem of Judah
>   to the remote hill country of Ephraim.
> > (19:18a, RSV*)

Next he reports only his origin and destiny:

> From there I [came].
> Then I went to Bethlehem of Judah.
> Now to my house I am going.[32]
> > (19:18b)

At last, he returns to the present, without acknowledging his companions. "No man takes *me* into his house" (19:18c). The words alter even as they echo narrated discourse (19:15b).[33] The master continues to talk. Needing a place to spend the night, he assures the old man that the travelers will not burden him:

> Also straw and provender there is for our asses;
> also bread and wine there is for me and for your maidservant
>   and for the attendant with your servant.
> There is no need of anything.
> > (19:19)

Is the master speaking the truth or is he feigning provisions to improve his chances for overnight lodging? Two ingratiating touches arouse suspicion. He refers to his own concubine as the old man's property, thereby offering her as bait; he demeans himself (or perhaps the entire party) in the phrase "your servant(s)," thereby flattering the old man.[34] Whatever the truth, these inventions work. The master gets what he wants. The old man said:[35]

> Shalom to you.
> I entirely (*raq*) will care for all your needs.
> Only (*raq*) do not spend the night in the square.
> > (19:20, RSV*)

Concluding this episode, the narrator mitigates the danger stated at the beginning. "No man took (*'sp*) them into his house to spend the night" (19:15b) yields to "so he brought (*bô'*) him into his house" (19:21a, RSV). The switch from the plural *them* to the singular *him* echoes the master's language (19:18c). It is also prophetic. Though the master is safe in the house, the woman is not. For the time being, however, the travelers wash their feet and eat and drink.[36] The old man gives the donkeys provender (19:21).[37] Hospitality prevails. Yet safety within the house cannot control danger without.

B. *Episode Two, 19:22–28.* The second episode of scene two begins in the house, shifts outside, and then returns. These three movements organize its content. A distinctive feature is the play on the words *house* (*byt*), *door* (*dlt*), and *doorway* (*pth*). Continuing its thematic journey throughout the story, the term *house* occurs in each of the three sections of this episode. Altogether new, the words *door* and *doorway* alternate in the first and second sections but appear together in the third. Symbolically, the door or doorway marks the boundary between hospitality and hostility. Throughout this night of violence, only the female crosses the boundary; the males make sure of that.

1. *Within the house, 19:22–25b.* Structured with narration surrounding direct discourse, the first section opens with a party. Inside the house, the travelers "are enjoying (*yṭb*) themselves to their heart" (19:22), a phrase that recalls the days of hospitality in Bethlehem when the girl's father urged the master to "let your heart be merry" (*yṭb*; 19:6, 9). In turn, this recollection leads back to the motive of the master in going to Bethlehem: "to speak to the heart of his concubine" (19:3). Thus far in the story he has spoken to her not at all. Instead, he has directed his attention to other males: his father-in-law, his attendant, and now the old man from his home territory.

In the midst of this festive occasion,

> suddenly (*hinnēh*) men of the city,
>> men of the sons of wickedness,
> surround the house, pounding on the door;
> and they shout to the man, the lord of the house,
>> the old man.

> (19:22)

Danger knocks at the door of merriment. The extended descriptions of the two groups presage their struggle. The men of Gibeah are "men of the sons of wickedness";[38] the old man is "the lord (*ba'al*) of the house." Male power confronts male power. "Bring out the man who came to your house that we may know him" (19:22e, RSV). Though the phrase "to know him" may itself be ambiguous,[39] on the lips of wicked men it bodes the worst. They wish to violate the guest sexually. The man, the lord of the house, replies decisively,[40] "No, my brothers." The vocative is ironic, used perhaps to mollify them. Then he continues, encircling his male guest with the protection of prohibitions:

> Do not act so wickedly;
>   seeing that this man has come into my house,
> do not do this vile thing (*nĕbālāh*).[41]
>
> (19:23, RSV)

But the lord of the house can do more than forbid. He can offer an alternative. To counterbalance prohibition he grants permission. He even accents the positive by introducing his suggestion with the emphatic Hebrew word *hinnēh*: "Look, now," he exclaims, "my daughter the virgin and his concubine!" (19:24). Two female objects he offers to protect a male from a group of wicked "brothers." One of these women is bone of his bones and flesh of his flesh, his very own daughter. The other belongs to his guest. Moreover, these two females can satisfy the gamut of heterosexual preferences. One is virgin property; the other, seasoned and experienced. Both are expendable to the demands of wicked men. In fact, the lord of the house will himself give these women away. "Let me bring them out," he offers.[42] The male protector becomes procurer. Further, just as he has used two negative imperatives to defend his male guest, so he employs two positive commands to imperil his female captives:

> Ravish them,
> and do to them the good in your eyes.
>
> (19:24)

No restrictions whatsoever does this lord place upon the use of the two women. Instead, he gives wicked men a license to rape them. His final words of negative command emphasize again the point of it all. "But to this man do not do this vile thing" (*nĕbālāh*; 19:24). If done to a man, such an act is a vile thing; if done to women, it is "the good" in the eyes of men.[43] Thus the old man mediates between males to give each side what it wants. No male is to be violated. All males, even wicked ones, are to be granted their wishes. Conflict among them can be solved by the sacrifice of females.

To those familiar with the traditions of ancient Israel, terrible memories surface. Once upon a time two messengers came to the city of Sodom to visit Lot, who, similar to our old man, was a so-journer, not a native (Gen. 19:1–29).[44] Lot persuaded these strangers to enter his home.[45] Feasting followed, and then they prepared for bed. At that moment, the men of Sodom, from youngest to oldest, surrounded the house. While the wicked men of Gibeah constitute only a part of the male citizenry, all the men of Sodom demanded that Lot turn over the guests "that we may know them" (Gen. 19:5).

Just as the old Ephraimite goes out to talk to those who pound on his door (Judg. 19:23), so Lot went out of his door to speak to these men (Gen. 19:6). The words of the two hosts are virtually identical. Lot implored, "I beg you, my brothers, do not act so wickedly" (Gen. 19:7, RSV). Then he offered an alternative. "Look, now (*hinnēh*), I have two daughters who have not known a man" (Gen. 19:8; cf. Judg. 19:24). If the old man can offer one virgin who is his own flesh and blood, Lot could promise two. And like the old man, Lot the father would give his daughters away. "Let me bring them out to you," he said (Gen. 19:8, RSV). Then followed one positive command to match his earlier negative prohibition. "Do to them according to the good in your own eyes." Again, the language heralded the words of our old man. Moreover, Lot's conclusion underscored the point of it all. "Only do nothing to these men, for they have come under the shelter of my roof" (Gen. 19:8, RSV). Like the old man in Gibeah, Lot tried to mediate between males, giving each side what it wanted. No male was to be violated. All males were to be granted their wishes. Conflict among them could be solved by the sacrifice of females. The male protector, indeed the father, became procurer.

These two stories show that rules of hospitality in Israel protect only males. Though Lot entertained men alone, the old man also has a female guest, and no hospitality safeguards her. She is chosen as the victim for male lust. Further, in neither of these stories does the male host offer himself in place of his guests. Constant only is the use of innocent and helpless women to guard and gratify men of all sorts. Nonetheless, Lot's proposal was rejected, not out of concern for his virgin daughters but out of animosity that a sojourner should try to adjudicate the crisis (Gen. 19:9). Ironically, male anger against another male spared Lot's daughters the horrors for which he had volunteered them. Similarly, one line in our story reports the dissatisfaction of the Benjaminites with the proposal of the old man. "But the men would not listen to him" (19:25a, RSV).[46] This time, however, male anger does not spare the female.

Parallel in setting, vocabulary, and motifs, the two stories now diverge to make ours the more despicable. Nothing has prepared us for the terror to come. Dialogue stops; bargaining ceases; the old man and his virgin daughter disappear. No one waits to learn what the dissatisfied Benjaminites might propose next. Instead, a non sequitur follows the comment of the narrator that the men would not listen to the old man. "And the man," that is our master, the overnight guest, "seized (ḥzq) his concubine and pushed to them outside" (19:25b).[47] So hurried is his action that the Hebrew omits the direct object her for the second verb. The one whom the storyteller earlier portrayed sympathetically, seeking out his concubine "to speak to her heart," turns her over to the enemy to save himself. Truly, the hour is at hand, and the woman is betrayed into the hands of sinners (cf. Mark 14:41). At the end of this section, then, safety within the house has lost to danger without. Yet only the concubine suffers the loss. No one within comes to her aid. They have all fallen away in the darkness of night (cf. Mark 14:26–42). "And the man seized his concubine and pushed to them outside." Danger knocking at the door of merriment acquires its victim.

2. *Outside the house, 19:25c–26.* Pushing the concubine outside (haḥûṣ) marks the shift to the middle section of the episode. Through the distancing of narrated discourse, the tale of terror unfolds. The crime itself receives few words. If the storyteller advocates neither pornography nor sensationalism, he also cares little about the woman's fate. The brevity of this section on female rape contrasts sharply with the lengthy reports on male carousing and male deliberations that precede it. Such elaborate attention to men intensifies the terror perpetrated upon the woman. Reporting the crime, the narrator appropriates the vocabulary of the wicked men of the city who wished to know the male guest. "And they knew (ydꜥ) her" (19:25c). In this context "to know" loses all ambiguity. It means rape, and it parallels a verb connoting ruthless abuse. "And they raped (ydꜥ) her and tortured (ꜥll) her all night until the morning" (19:25d).[48] These third-person plural verbs and the time reference guarantee that the crime was not a single deed but rather multiple acts of violence. "They raped her and tortured her all night until the morn-

ing." A third verb completes their action. "And they let her go as the dawn came up" (19:25e). Raped, tortured, and released: brevity of speech discloses the extravagance of violence.

Strikingly, the next action belongs to the woman herself.

> The woman came at daybreak
>   and fell down at the doorway
>   of the house of the man
>   where her master was until light.
> (19:26)

For the first time since the beginning of the story, the lone female is the subject of active verbs, though she is no longer a subject with power to act. Instead, she is the violated property of the master who betrayed her. Once she left this man, but he reclaimed her only to deliver her into the hands of other men who beat on the door (*dlt*) of the house (19:22). Now that they have raped and discarded her outside (19:25d), she has no choice but to "fall down at the doorway (*ptḥ*) of the house." Her physical state embodies her servile position. Meanwhile, the master has remained safe within throughout the night. Morning confronts him with the atrocity that he initiated.

Contrasts between darkness and light enhance the ironies of the situation. Juxtaposed to the single phrase "all night," four references accent the coming of the day:

> They tortured her all night <u>until the morning.</u>
> (19:25c)
> They let her go <u>when the dawn came up.</u>
> (19:25d)
>
> The woman came <u>at daybreak</u>
> and fell down . . . <u>until light.</u>
> (19:26)

Daybreak exposes the crime and its aftermath. Rather than dispelling the darkness, the light of morning presages its overwhelming presence. Perversely, the discovery of the crime leads to further violence against the woman. For it, the master alone is responsible. Though the men of Gibeah raped the concubine all night, he will perform his despicable deed "in the morning" (19:27).

3. *At the door of the house and away, 19:27–28.* In the final section of this episode, the devastated woman succumbs to the will of the master. Form and content demonstrate his power and her plight.

Predominantly narration, the section begins with the master's resolve to leave. But the appearance of the woman interrupts. Only
then come words of direct discourse—his, not hers. At the close,
the man resumes his way, having fit her into his plans. Artfully
constructed, the unit builds on themes and vocabulary from the preceding sections, while organizing itself through the placement of the
verbs *arise* (*qûm*) and *go* (*hlk*) at the beginning, middle, and end.

   a. *Resolve*

     Now her master <u>arose</u> in the morning,
       and he opened <u>(*pṭḥ*)</u> the door (*dlt*) of the house (*byt*)
       and he went out <u>to go</u> on his way.

   b. *Interruption*

     But, behold (*hinnēh*), there was the woman his concubine,
       having fallen at the doorway (*pṭḥ*) of the house (*byt*),
       her hands upon the threshold.
     And he said to her,
       '<u>Arise</u> and <u>let us be going</u> .'
     But there was no answer.

   c. *Resumption*

     Then he put her upon the ass,
       and the man <u>rose up</u> and <u>he went away</u> to his place.
                         (19:27–28, RSV*)

At the beginning of this unit, the phrase, "in the morning," continues
the time references of section two (19:25, 26). The words *door, doorway*, and *house* echo from both sections one and two. Indeed, by
using the word for *door* (*dlt*) that appeared in the first and the word
for *doorway* (*pṭḥ*) in the second, the final section underscores the
boundary that the master has managed to observe while forcing his
concubine to transgress.

"Now her master arose in the morning, and he opened the door
of the house and he went out to go on his way." The text reads as
though he intended to depart alone without regard for anyone else.
And why not? By manipulation and force he has gotten what he
wanted, even though all that he feared has come to pass inversely.
He set danger on the road at night over against safety in a town,
but it was not so; danger in a foreign city over against safety among
his own people, but it was not so; danger in the open square over

against safety in a house, but it was not so. Nevertheless, he saved himself through an act of cowardice that transferred the danger to his concubine. Now the master must face the victim.

"Behold, there was the woman his concubine, having fallen at the doorway of the house, her hands upon the threshold." The Hebrew word *hinnēh* introduces the female presence. The two nouns "the woman his concubine" indicate her inferior position. The phrase "having fallen at the doorway of the house" dramatizes her pain and powerlessness. And the touching detail "her hands upon the threshold" secures her plight.

Having returned the woman to the threshold of safety, the narrator keeps her outside. A poignant image yields cruel irony. Will this woman, violated and discarded, elicit compassion or remorse from her master? Two Hebrew words give the answer. "Arise," he orders, addressing her for the first and only time. "Let-us-be-going." Where are the words that speak to her heart? Certainly not here. Nowhere in the story has the portrayal of the master even hinted that he might fulfill the narrator's description of his intention. Instead, he forces the woman to fit his plans.

"'Arise and let us be going.' But there was no answer." Is she dead or alive? The Greek Bible says, "for she was dead," and hence makes the men of Benjamin murderers as well as rapists and torturers. The Hebrew text, on the other hand, is silent, allowing the interpretation that this abused woman is yet alive.[49] Oppressed and tortured, she opens not her mouth. Like a lamb that is led to the slaughter, and like a sheep before its shearers is dumb, so she opens not her mouth. "'Arise and let us be going.' But there was no answer." Her silence, be it exhaustion or death, deters the master not at all. What he set out to do in the light of the morning, he does. Putting her upon the donkey, "the man rose up and he went away to his place." No words describe the journey. His mission is completed, though not as the narrator proposed it.

CONTINUING VIOLENCE

Conclusion: Judges 19:29–30

With radically altered lenses, the conclusion of the story plays upon the introduction (19:1–2). As the narrative began in the hill country of Ephraim with the Levite but then moved away with the concubine to her father's house in Bethlehem of Judah (19:1–2), so the closing verses begin in the house of the master in Ephraim (19:29abc) and then move away with the concubine into all the territory of Israel (19:29d–30). But the differences between beginning and ending yield terror. The live concubine who once left her master has become the dead object of his appalling violence. Her movement away from him now is actually his call for revenge.

Arriving at his house,[50] the master wastes no time. In rapid succession, four verbs describe his activities: took, seized, cut, and sent. "He took (*lqḥ*) the knife"—not a knife but *the* knife (19:29a). How provocative is this sentence because it echoes a line from the sacrifice of Isaac. "Then Abraham . . . took (*lqḥ*) the knife" (Gen. 22:10). In all of scripture only these two stories share that precise vocabulary. Yet Abraham took the knife explicitly "to slay his son." Perhaps that intention can be stated because it did not happen; an angel stopped the murder of Isaac. The master also "took the knife." Does he intend to slay the concubine? Though the Greek Bible rules out such a possibility, the silence of the Hebrew text allows it. Moreover, the unique parallel to the action of Abraham encourages it. Perhaps the purpose in taking the knife, to slay the victim, is not specified here because indeed it does happen. The narrator, however, protects his protagonist through ambiguity.

"He took the knife and he seized (*ḥzq*) his concubine." Raped, tortured, and dead or alive, this woman is still in the power of her master. Her battered body evokes escalated brutality from him. No agent, human or divine, intervenes. Instead, the knife, symbol of a terror that faith once prevented, now prevails. Earlier the master had "seized (*ḥzq*) his concubine and pushed to them outside" (19:25b); this time he himself completes the violence. "He cut her (*ntḥ*), limb by limb, into twelve pieces and sent her (*šlḥ*) throughout all the territory of Israel" (19:29c).[51] Is the cowardly betrayer also the murderer? Certainly no mourning becomes the man; no burial attends the woman.

Of all the characters in scripture, she is the least. Appearing at the beginning and close of a story that rapes her, she is alone in a world of men. Neither the other characters nor the narrator recognizes her humanity. She is property, object, tool, and literary device. Without name, speech, or power, she has no friends to aid her in life or mourn her in death. Passing her back and forth among themselves, the men of Israel have obliterated her totally. Captured, betrayed, raped, tortured, murdered, dismembered, and scattered—this woman is the most sinned against.[52] In the end, she is no more than the oxen that Saul will later cut (*ntḥ*) in pieces and send (*šlḥ*) throughout all the territory of Israel as a call to war (1 Sam. 11:7).[53] Her body has been broken and given to many. Lesser power has no woman than this, that her life is laid down by a man.

As the fragments of the body of this nameless woman scatter throughout the land of Israel, the singular horror presses its claims upon the people.[54] According to the Greek Bible, the master instructs the messengers who carry the bits and pieces to say: "Thus you shall say to every man [not generic] of Israel, 'Has there ever been such a deed as this[55] from the time the Israelites came up from the land of Egypt to this day?'" The Hebrew Bible, on the other hand, omits both messengers and message to have Israel, in effect, answer the question before it is posed. Hence, the RSV reads, "And all who saw it said, 'Such a thing has never happened or been seen from the day that the people of Israel came up out of the land of Egypt until this day'" (19:30).[56]

Yet the declaration in Hebrew contains a nuance that English translations cannot preserve. The verbal forms and the object are all feminine gender. Hebrew has no neuter. The feminine gender can accent the woman herself, not just this abstract or collective "thing" that has happened. Literally, we may translate, "And all who saw *her* said, '*She* was not, and *she* was not seen such as this from the day that the people came up out of the land of Egypt until this day.'" In other words, the ambiguity of the grammatical forms serves a particular hermeneutical emphasis: to highlight the woman who is the victim of terror. The commands that follow enhance the point.

In both versions, the Greek and the Hebrew, three imperatives instruct Israel: consider, take counsel, and speak. Strikingly, the first command is actually the Hebrew idiom, "direct your heart," followed by the phrase "to her." Translations yield such readings as "consider it" (RSV), "put your mind to this" (NJV), or even the casual "take note of it" (NAB). Thereby both the feminine object and the play on the imagery of heart disappear. Long ago the man was supposed to speak to the heart of the woman, though he did not. Now Israel must direct its heart toward her, take counsel, and speak. Act One of the Benjaminite traditions concludes with an imperative to respond.

RESPONSES TO THE STORY

From Tribal Israel. Acts Two (Judges 20) and Three (Judges 21) constitute an immediate response. All the people from Dan to Beersheba gather as "one man (*'îš*) . . . to the Lord at Mizpah." Clearly this answer will be extravagant. Even God, who has been absent altogether from the preceding act, participates as four hundred thousand soldiers demand an explanation from the Levite.

His reply (20:4–7, RSV) begins in a straightforward way. "I came to Gibeah that belongs to Benjamin, I and my concubine, to spend the night. And the men of Gibeah rose against me and beset the house round about me by night." Then the master continues with an interpretation that departs from the stated intentions of the men of Gibeah: "They meant to kill me." They had asked, instead, to "know" him. Even if the Levite's understanding of their request is legitimate, his next words obscure the truth. "They meant to kill me, and they ravished my concubine, and she is dead." Omitted altogether is the contribution of the Levite, who had seized and given her to the men. By the crime of silence he absolves himself. Moreover, his carefully phrased admission, "she is dead," rather than, "they killed her," reinforces the suspicion that he is murderer as well as betrayer.[57] The dismemberment of the concubine the Levite readily reports as his own deed. "And I took my concubine and cut her in pieces, and I sent her throughout all the country of the inheritance of Israel; for they have committed abomination and wantonness in Israel." Certainly, the Levite fears no retribution for having mutilated the body of this woman. That act is an acceptable call to revenge. Hence, the wrath of all Israel turns against the Benjaminites. Outrage erupts at the harm done to a man through his property but ignores the violence done against the woman herself. Once more, having gotten what he wanted, the Levite leaves the story.

Subsequently, the tribes of Israel demand that Benjamin give up the wicked men of Gibeah so that "we may put them to death and put away evil from Israel" (20:13, RSV). But the Benjaminites refuse, and the battle begins.[58] In great detail, the narrator describes a conflict of incredible proportions. Thousands and thousands of men participate. Yahweh also joins the fight against Benjamin. After two initial defeats, the tribes gain victory by a ruse. Carnage is everywhere. Over twenty-five thousand men of Benjamin perish in a day. First the city of Gibeah and then all the towns of Benjamin go up in smoke. Not a single woman (21:16), child, or beast survives (20:48). The tribe of Benjamin is virtually annihilated, only six hundred men having escaped to the wilderness.

This gigantic outpouring of violence causes second thoughts. The victors cannot live with the reality that "there should be today one tribe lacking in Israel" (21:3, RSV). To replenish itself, the tribe of Benjamin must have women for the six hundred male survivors. One oath complicates and a second resolves the problem. Having vowed not to give their own daughters in marriage to Benjamin (21:1), the other tribes have also sworn to destroy anyone who failed to help in the war (21:5). Accordingly, they attack the derelict town of Jabesh-gilead, murdering all the inhabitants except four hundred young virgins (21:10–12). These females they turn over to the male remnant of Benjamin, just as the Levite once turned the concubine over to the wicked men of Benjamin. The rape of one has become the rape of four hundred. Still the Benjaminites are unsatisfied because four hundred women cannot meet the demands of six hundred soldiers. This time the daughters of Shiloh must pay the price. To gratify the lust of males, the men of Israel sanction the abduction of two hundred young women as they come out to dance in the yearly festival of Yahweh (21:23). In total, the rape of one has become the rape of six hundred.

Entrusted to Israelite men, the story of the concubine justifies the expansion of violence against women. What these men claim to abhor, they have reenacted with vengeance. They have captured, betrayed, raped, and scattered four hundred virgins of Jabesh-gilead and two hundred daughters of Shiloh. Furthermore, they have tortured and murdered all the women of Benjamin and all the married women of Jabesh-gilead. Israelite males have dismembered the corporate body of Israelite females. Inasmuch as men have done it unto

one of the least of women, they have done it unto many. Tribal
Israel failed to direct its heart to the concubine.

From the Editor of Judges. A second response comes from the editor
of the book of Judges, whose voice merges with that of the narrator.
At the beginning of Act One, he indicted the age thus: "In those
days, there was no king in Israel." Now, at the conclusion of Act
Three, he repeats this judgment and adds: "Every man did what
was right in his own eyes."[59] The phrase, "in his own eyes," plays
on the words of the old man to the wicked men of Gibeah: "Do to
them [the virgin daughter and the concubine] the good in your own
eyes" (19:24). The lack of a king is a license for anarchy and violence. So the editor uses the horrors he has just reported to promote
a monarchy that would establish order and justice in Israel.[60] Concluding not only this story but the entire book of Judges with an
indictment, he prepares his readers to look favorably upon kingship.
What irony, then, that the first king, Saul, should come from the
tribe of Benjamin, establish his capital in Gibeah, and deliver Jabesh-
gilead from the Ammonites![61] But undercutting Saul to advocate the
Davidic monarchy may be precisely what the editor intends. The
reign of David, however, brings its own atrocities. David pollutes
Bathsheba; Amnon rapes Tamar; and Absalom violates the concubines of his father.[62] In those days there was a king in Israel, and
royalty did the right in its own eyes. Clearly, to counsel a political
solution to the story of the concubine is ineffectual. Such a perspective does not direct its heart to her.

From the Shapers of the Canon. Yet a third set of responses arises
from the canonical orderings of the scriptures. It is the response by
juxtaposition. In the Hebrew Bible, the story of Hannah follows
immediately the story of the concubine (1 Sam. 1:1—2:21).[63] Though
also set in the hill country of Ephraim, with travel elsewhere, this
narrative depicts a different world inhabited by different characters:
Elkanah, the loving husband who attends to the grief of his barren
wife Hannah; Eli, the honorable priest who blesses the woman and
seeks divine favor for her; Yahweh, the gracious deity who answers
her tears and prayers with fertility; and Samuel, the special child
who honors his mother by ministering to the Lord at Shiloh.

Throughout the story, Hannah receives sympathetic and focused attention. She is a woman of name and speech, piety and perseverance, fidelity and magnanimity. The male characters and the narrator highlight her worth and her faith. And all this belongs to the days of the judges. What a contrast is the treatment of Hannah to that of the concubine!

Similarly, the response by juxtaposition occurs in the Greek Bible. There the story of Ruth follows immediately the story of the concubine. Like scene one of this narrative, the book of Ruth is set in Bethlehem. It too is a study in hospitality, but this time a female version.[64] Through its women, the whole town greets the widow Naomi upon her return from Moab with Ruth, her foreign daughter-in-law. Under the blessing of God, these two women work out their own salvation. The patriarch Boaz cooperates by providing sustenance and marrying Ruth. When the benevolent elders of Bethlehem threaten to subsume the concerns of these females to male perspectives, the women reclaim their narrative. They reinterpret the language of a man's world to preserve the integrity of a woman's story. The son born to Ruth restores life to Naomi rather than the name of the dead Elimelech to his inheritance. In naming this male child, the women of Bethlehem make a new beginning with men. And all this happens "in the days when the judges ruled" (Ruth 1:1). What a contrast is the treatment of Ruth and Naomi to that of the concubine!

The absence of misogyny, violence, and vengeance in the two stories juxtaposed to the Benjaminite traditions speaks a healing word in the days of the judges. The portrayal of the women enhances the message. Alongside the concubine, the women of Benjamin, the young women of Jabesh-gilead, and the daughters of Shiloh stand Hannah, Naomi, Ruth, and the women of Bethlehem. Though the presence of the latter group cannot erase the sufferings of their sisters, it does show both the Almighty and the male establishment a more excellent way. To direct the heart of these stories to the concubine, then, is to counsel redemption.

From the Prophets. Within scripture, a fourth response to the story comes from the prophetic literature, specifically from Hosea. Two passing references suggest that memories of Gibeah lingered for centuries.[65] In announcing days of punishment for Israel, the prophet declares:

> They have deeply corrupted themselves
>   as in the days of Gibeah.
> God will remember their iniquity;
>   God will punish their sins.
> (Hos. 9:9, RSV*)

A second time he says:

> From the days of Gibeah,
>   you have sinned, O Israel.
> (Hos. 10:9, RSV)

Two allusions are meager memories for the crimes of Gibeah. The prophetic tradition scarcely directed its heart to the concubine.

From the Rest of Scripture. Overwhelming silence is the fifth response to this text. It comes from both ancient Israel and the early Christian community. If the Levite failed to report the whole story to the tribes of Israel, how much more has the canonical tradition failed to remember it. The biting, even sarcastic, words of the prophet Amos on another occasion capture well the spirit of this response:

> Therefore, the prudent one will keep silent
>   about such a time,
> for it is an evil time.
> (Amos 5:13, RSV)

Silence covers impotence and complicity. To keep quiet is to sin, for the story orders its listeners to "direct your heart to her, take counsel, and speak" (19:30; 20:7).

From the Readers. "Direct your heart to her, take counsel, and speak." From their ancient setting, these imperatives move into the present, challenging us to answer anew. Thus, the sixth response awaits the readers of the story. Truly, to speak for this woman is to interpret against the narrator, plot, other characters, and the biblical tradition because they have shown her neither compassion nor attention. When we direct our hearts to her, what counsel can we take? What word can we speak? What can we, the heirs of Israel, say in the presence of such unrelenting and unredeemed terror?

First of all, we can recognize the contemporaneity of the story. Misogyny belongs to every age, including our own. Violence and vengeance are not just characteristics of a distant, pre-Christian past; they infect the community of the elect to this day. Woman as object is still captured, betrayed, raped, tortured, murdered, dismembered, and scattered. To take to heart this ancient story, then, is to confess its present reality.[66] The story is alive, and all is not well. Beyond confession we must take counsel to say, "Never again." Yet this counsel is itself ineffectual unless we direct our hearts to that most uncompromising of all biblical commands, speaking the word not to others but to ourselves: Repent. Repent.[67]

NOTES

1. On the composition of Judges, see Robert G. Boling, *Judges,* Anchor Bible (Garden City, N.Y.: Doubleday & Co., 1975), pp. 29–38; idem, "'In Those Days There Was No King in Israel,'" in *A Light unto My Path,* ed. Howard N. Bream, Ralph D. Heim, and Carey A. Moore (Philadelphia: Temple University Press, 1974), pp. 33–48; J. Alberto Soggin, *Judges,* OTL (Philadelphia: Westminster Press, 1981), pp. 4–5.

2. Judg. 17:6a; 18:1a; 19:1a; 21:25a.

3. Judg. 17:6b; 21:25b.

4. Wherever they are not identified in this essay, chapter and verse citations come from the book of Judges.

5. The three acts are the story of the concubine (19:1b–30), of Israelite wars against Benjamin (20:1–48), and of the securing of wives for the Benjaminites (21:1–24). Cf. Martin Buber's description of this material as "put together from a baroque, overspread elaboration of a legendary theme . . . in a loquacious style . . . reported circumstantially and unclearly . . ." (*Kingship of God* [New York: Harper & Row, 1967], p. 78). For a study of this unit focused on the theme of community, see Susan Niditch, "The 'Sodomite' Theme in Judges 19—20: Family, Community, and Social Disintegration," *CBQ* 44 (1982): 365–78.

6. For a thorough analysis of this text, see, most recently, Hans-Winfried Jüngling, *Richter 19—Ein Plädoyer für das Königtum* (Rome: Biblical Institute Press, 1981).

7. *Contra* the RSV, I translate *n'r* as attendant, rather than as servant and/or young man, to differentiate it from *'bd* (servant) in 19:19.

8. See Raymond Abba, "Priests and Levites," *The Interpreter's Dictionary of the Bible* 3 (hereafter *IDB*), ed. George Arthur Buttrick (Nashville: Abingdon Press, 1962), pp. 876–89.

9. See Otto J. Baab, "Concubine," *IDB* 1, p. 666; Soggin, *Judges,* p. 159.

10. For discussions of these traditions, see the commentaries; e.g., George F. Moore, *A Critical and Exegetical Commentary on Judges,* ICC (Edinburgh: T. & T. Clark, 1976), pp. 409–10; C. F. Burney, *The Book of*

Judges (New York: KTAV Publishing House, 1970), pp. 459–61; Boling, *Judges*, pp. 273–74; Soggin, *Judges*, p. 284.

11. Throughout I shall call the Levite "the master" to distinguish him from the other nameless males and to indicate his power over the concubine.

12. Jüngling compares the departure of the concubine from her master to Hagar's flight from Sarai (Gen. 16:6). He observes also the uniqueness of the concubine's act in the traditions of Israel: she, not the man, initiates the separation. See *Richter 19*, pp. 87–90.

13. For a different analysis of the divisions in this scene, see Jüngling, *Richter 19*, pp. 90–152. Note especially his literary comparisons of the fourth and fifth days of the master's visit (pp. 115–18).

14. On the preferability of the Qere *lahăšíbāh*, "to bring her back," see Moore, *Judges*, pp. 409–10; Burney, *Judges*, p. 461.

15. On this instance of retardation, see Jacob Licht, *Storytelling in the Bible* (Jerusalem: Magnes Press, 1978), pp. 106–7.

16. Boling observes the *inclusio* formed around the visit by the phrase, "his father-in-law, the father of the young woman," in 19:4a and 9 (*Judges*, p. 274). On the graciousness of the greeting, cf. Jüngling's comments on the verb, "made him stay" (*Richter 19*, pp. 106–8).

17. *Contra* Soggin, *Judges*, p. 285, the phrase "spent the night" (19:4, 6b, 9b) is not "a euphemism for the resumption of matrimonial relations." Male bonding is the point; see below on 19:5–7.

18. Like Abraham who entertained three strangers in his tent at Mamre, the father plays down his generosity by the phrase, "Strengthen your heart with a morsel of bread" (cf. Gen. 18:4–5). Further, like Abraham, he pictures the delay as an aid to departure.

19. For this interpretation of the Hebrew *htmhmhw* in 19:8, see Boling, *Judges*, pp. 87, 275.

20. On the varieties of meaning for *hinnēh*, see Thomas O. Lambdin, *Introduction to Biblical Hebrew* (New York: Charles Scribner's Sons, 1971), pp. 168–71; C. J. Labuschagne, "The Particles הֵן and הִנֵּה," *Syntax and Meaning: Studies in Hebrew Syntax and Biblical Exegesis*, Oudtestamentische Studiën 18, ed. A. S. van der Woude (Leiden: E. J. Brill, 1973), pp. 1–4.

21. Note again the father's expression, "Let your heart be merry" (19:9).

22. In the three time periods of this episode, power has passed from the father (19:4) to the two males joined equally (19:6) to the master (19:8–10).

23. Cf. Boling, *Judges*, p. 274: "It was a man's world. There is no mention of the interest of the girl [*sic*] in rejoining her husband, nor of what the womenfolk did while the two men celebrated for most of a week."

24. On Jebus, see Soggin, *Judges*, p. 286; Jüngling, *Richter 19*, pp. 147–48.

25. For a stylistic analysis of the conversation, see Jüngling, *Richter 19*, pp. 162–70. Note his comparison (following W. Richter) with the story of the daughter of Jephthah, especially with Judg. 11:34a–40. On the Jephthah story, see chapter 4 below.

26. On the place names, see Soggin, *Judges*, pp. 286–87.

27. The word *saga* here means story.

28. If one counts the two occurrences of the name Bethlehem, then the word house (*byt*) occurs four times in the middle (19:18).

29. Note that the master alone is the subject of active verbs; those traveling with him are explicitly included only as objects of the verb *took*.

30. On ironies in the story, see Stuart D. Currie, "Judges 19—21: Biblical Studies for a Seminar on Sexuality and the Human Community," *Austin Seminary Bulletin* 87 (1971): 14.

31. Cf. the similar question asked of Hagar (Gen. 16:8); see Jüngling, *Richter 19*, pp. 185–86.

32. On the difficulties of the Hebrew text, see Moore, *Judges*, pp. 415–16. Cf. "house" here with "tent" in 19:9; see Boling, *Judges*, p. 276.

33. On the interplay of narration and direct speech, see Alter, *The Art of Biblical Narrative* (New York: Basic Books, 1981), pp. 63–87.

34. Though the preponderant textual evidence is for the singular "your servant," the plural "your servants" is not inappropriate. The precise meaning of the phrases "your maidservant" and "your servant" is uncertain, but their context suggests that the master is speaking of his concubine and himself. Altogether his references include the entire party (master, concubine, attendant, and animals). Cf. Boling, *Judges*, pp. 275–76.

35. Note the brevity of the two speeches of the old man (19:17b and 19:20) as they surround the longer discourse of the master (19:18–19). Cf. this discourse with the silence of the master in scene one (19:3–10). In both instances the master prevails over another male. On the particle *raq* in 19:20, see B. Jongeling, "La Particle רק," *Syntax and Meaning*, Oudtestamentische Studiën 18, ed. A. S. van der Woude (Leiden: E. J. Brill, 1973), pp. 97–107.

36. Note the structural parallel between this narrated ending (19:21) and the ending of the master's speech in 19:18c–19. In each case discourse continues beyond a repeated phrase that might otherwise signal the conclusion of the unit: "Nobody takes me into his house" (19:18c) and "so he brought him into his house" (19:21a).

37. This report increases the suspicions raised in 19:19 about the master providing provender. On the other hand, it may testify to the generosity of the old man.

38. On the phrase, "sons of wickedness," see Burney, *Judges*, pp. 467–69; Boling, *Judges*, p. 276; Jüngling, *Richter 19*, pp. 199–203.

39. See Boling, *Judges*, p. 276.

40. Though the text says, "he went out to them" (19:23), it does not use the dangerous symbols for exit, *door* and *doorway*. The old man is safe both outside and in.

41. Cf. the reply of Tamar to Amnon (2 Sam. 13:12–13); see chapter 2, note 34 above. For this and other thematic and verbal links between 2 Samuel 13 and Judges 19—21, see R. A. Carlson, *David, the Chosen King: A Traditio-Historical Approach to the Second Book of Samuel* (Stockholm: Almqvist & Wiksell, 1964), pp. 165–67. On *nĕbālāh*, see further Currie, "Judges 19—21" p. 19; also Jüngling, *Richter 19*, pp. 211–17.

42. On the apparent grammatical anomaly of masculine pronouns, see Boling, *Judges*, p. 276.

43. Cf. the use of the idiom, "the good in your eyes," in reference to the affliction of Hagar (Gen. 16:6); also the numerous sexual references to eyes in the story of Tamar (e.g., 2 Sam. 13:2, 5b, 6b, 8); cf. Gen. 19:8 below.

44. Many scholars argue for the dependence of Judges 19 upon Genesis 19. See, e.g., Moore, *Judges*, pp. 417–19; Burney, *Judges*, pp. 443–44; Soggin, *Judges*, pp. 282, 288; Robert C. Culley, *Studies in the Structure of Hebrew Narrative* (Philadelphia: Fortress Press, 1976), pp. 56–59. See also D. M. Gunn, "Narrative Patterns and Oral Tradition in Judges and Samuel," *VT* 24 (1974): 294, especially note 1. (I have not had access to the article by A. van den Born.) But cf. Niditch, "The 'Sodomite' Theme in Judges 19—20," pp. 375–78, who argues for the primacy of Judges 19 over Genesis 19. Yet another approach views such stories as type-scenes that move between fixed conventions and flexible appropriations, without specific literary dependence (cf. Alter, *The Art of Biblical Narrative*, pp. 47–62). For recent discussions of these stories, see Tom Horner, *Jonathan Loved David: Homosexuality in Biblical Times* (Philadelphia: Westminster Press, 1978), pp. 47–58 and John Boswell, *Christianity, Social Tolerance, and Homosexuality* (Chicago: University of Chicago Press, 1980), pp. 92–98.

45. Unlike any inhabitant of Gibeah, Lot ran out to meet the strangers, insisting that they spend the night in his house and enjoy his hospitality. At first the travelers refused, declaring that they would spend the night in the street. Hence, their desire was the reverse of the wish of the master from Ephraim.

46. Cf. Amnon's narrated response to the words of Tamar (2 Sam. 13:14a, 16b); see Jüngling, *Richter 19*, pp. 217–20.

47. On this translation of Judg. 19:25b, see the NJV. Cf. the prominence of the verb *seize* (*ḥzq*) in the story of Tamar (2 Sam. 13:11, 14b).

48. On the verb *torture* (*'ll*), cf. 1 Sam. 31:4; Jer. 38:19; Num. 22:29.

49. For an excellent discussion of the ambiguity, see Robert Polzin, *Moses and the Deuteronomist* (New York: Seabury Press, 1980), pp. 200–202.

50. The occurrence of the word *house* revives the motif of competition between the master and his father-in-law. Narrated discourse contrasts "the father's house" at the beginning (19:2) with the master's "house" at the end (19:29). Yet the father referred to the master's abode as a "tent" (19:9). The discrepancy between the terminology of the narrator and the father suggests that "tent" was the sarcastic term (*contra* Boling, *Judges*, p. 276).

51. This verb *divide* is used elsewhere in scripture only for animals. Cf. the use of the verb *send* (*šlḥ*) in the story of Tamar (2 Sam. 13:16–17).

52. In an unpublished paper entitled, "Intricacy, Design, and Cunning in the Book of Judges," E. T. A. Davidson offers some illuminating parallels between the story of the concubine and other narratives in Judges that exhibit the themes of father-daughter and husband-wife, viz., the story of Caleb, Achsah, and Othniel (1:11–15); of Jephthah and his daughter (11:29–40); and of the Timnite and her father (14:20—15:8). She suggests that the placing of the concubine story at the end of the book completes an artistic progression from domestic tranquillity (1:11–15) to utter degradation. The progression symbolizes the story of premonarchic Israel itself. Indeed, the concubine is Israel ravished and cut apart.

53. For a comparison of Judg. 19:29 and 1 Sam. 11:7, see Jüngling, *Richter 19*, pp. 236–40. Cf. Soggin, *Judges*, p. 289; also Alan D. Crown, "Tidings

and Instructions: How News Travelled in the Ancient Near East," *Journal of the Economic and Social History of the Orient* 17 (1974): especially 253–54.

54. Thus, the ending contrasts with the corresponding section of the introduction (19:2). Rather than reporting the destination of the concubine, narrated discourse gives way to direct speech from all of Israel.

55. On meanings of "this," (19:30), see Currie, "Judges 19—21," p. 17; also Gerhard Wallis, "Eine Parallele zu Richter 19:29ff und 1. Sam. 11:5ff. aus dem Briefarchiv von Mari," *ZAW* 64 (1952): 57–61.

56. See Jüngling, *Richter 19*, pp. 240–44.

57. Yet the narrator continues to protect his protagonist through ambiguity. Note in 20:4a the description, "the man, the Levite, husband of the woman who was murdered," that again leaves unspecified the identity of the murderer. Cf. Licht, *Storytelling in the Bible*, pp. 78–79.

58. On this response as holy war, see Currie, "Judges 19—21," pp. 18–20; Polzin, *Moses and the Deuteronomist*, pp. 202–4; Niditch, "The 'Sodomite' Theme," pp. 371–75.

59. Although such a process of decision making may have worked for the good in an earlier time (cf. Deut. 12:8), in this context the words hold a negative meaning. For opposing interpretations, see Boling, *Judges*, p. 293; W. J. Dumbrell, " 'In Those Days There Was No King In Israel; Every Man Did What Was Right In His Own Eyes.' The Purpose of the Book of Judges Reconsidered," *JSOT* 25 (1983): 23–33.

60. See Martin Buber, *Kingship of God*, pp. 77–80; Jüngling, *Richter 19*, pp. 244–96.

61. 1 Sam. 9:1–2; 10:26; 11:1–11; 15:34; 22:6; 23:19.

62. 2 Sam. 11:2–27; 13:1–22; 16:20–23.

63. For literary readings of the story of Hannah, see Zvi Adar, *The Biblical Narrative* (Jerusalem: Department of Education and Culture of the World Zionist Organisation, 1959), pp. 19–28; Licht, *Storytelling in the Bible*, pp. 90–91, 114–115; Alter, *The Art of Biblical Narrative*, pp. 81–86.

64. For a literary reading, see Phyllis Trible, *God and the Rhetoric of Sexuality* (Philadelphia: Fortress Press, 1978), pp. 166–99.

65. For comments on these references, see Jüngling, *Richter 19*, pp. 280–84; also James Luther Mays, *Hosea*, OTL (Philadelphia: Westminster Press, 1969), pp. 131, 143; Hans Walter Wolff, *Hosea*, Hermeneia (Philadelphia: Fortress Press, 1974), pp. 158, 184.

66. See Dudley Clendinen, "Barroom Rape Shames Town of Proud Heritage," *New York Times*, 17 March 1983, sec. 1, p. A16. A summary of this article reports that "the rape of a 21-year-old woman in a New Bedford, Mass., bar has shocked the Northeast. The woman was hoisted to a pool table, tormented and repeatedly raped by a group of men who held her there for more than two hours while the other men in the tavern stood watching, sometimes taunting her and cheering. No one aided her or called the police" ("News Summary," *New York Times*, 17 March 1983, sec. 2, p. B1).

67. Repentance is a radical change in thinking that manifests itself in a radical change of behavior.

CHAPTER 4

THE
DAUGHTER
of JEPHTHAH

Virgin in Gilead

My God, my God,
why hast thou
forsaken her?

The Daughter of Jephthah
An Inhuman Sacrifice

Judges 11:29–40

Our final story also belongs to the days of the judges. Then Israel lived in tribal societies free from the power of a centralized government and yet subject to threats of anarchy and extinction.[1] Within this setting, public and private events interlocked to yield a saga of faithlessness, death, and mourning.[2]

In the cycle of tales about Jephthah the Gileadite,[3] our narrative constitutes scene two (11:29–40).[4] Preceding it are a theological preface (10:6–16), an introduction to the crises of the time (10:17—11:3), and a scene of partial resolution and continuing conflict (11:4–28). Following scene two is the conclusion of the cycle (13:1–7).[5] The second scene has two episodes plus a postscript. Episode one involves a public slaughter and episode two, a private sacrifice. The postscript memorializes the sacrifice. Our task is to study scene two with care for its central female character, the unnamed daughter of Jephthah.

THE CONTEXT OF SCENE TWO

A. *Introduction: The Juxtaposition of Crises, 10:17—11:3.* The introduction to the Jephthah cycle juxtaposes a public and a private crisis. In the eleventh century, when Ammon becomes a kingdom in Transjordan with Rabbah as its capital city, that nation begins to oppress the children of Israel, specifically those living in the territory of Gilead with Mizpah as their principal city.[6] For the Deuteronomic theologian, whose judgment prefaces the Jephthah cycle, this military threat is the work of the Lord. God is punishing Israel for its apostasy (10:6–16).[7] After confessing their sins, the children of Israel seek a deliverer, one to lead the fight against the Ammonites (10:17–18).[8]

Their savior emerges in ambiguity. "Now Jephthah the Gileadite was a mighty warrior" (11:1a, RSV), one well trained in combat who could supply his own equipment as well as a contingency of soldiers.[9] Beside these desirable credentials the storyteller places an irredeemable flaw: "But he (*hû'*) was the son of a prostitute" (11:1b). So uncertain was Jephthah's lineage that only the personified district of Gilead could qualify as his sire.[10] Child of an unnamed harlot and an unidentified father, Jephthah the mighty warrior suffered for the sins of his parents. The pure offspring of his generation expelled him from their father's house.[11] With an ironic touch, the narrator reports that Jephthah then fled "from his brothers" to dwell in the land of Tob (11:3a).[12] In time, this outcast attracts friends from the dregs of society. "Worthless fellows collected round Jephthah and went raiding with him (*'immô*)" (11:3b, RSV).[13] Truly, the savior has emerged in ambiguity.

B. *Scene One: Resolution and Reprisal, 11:4–28.* Having presented the future deliverer as an outcast, the storyteller proceeds to reunite Jephthah and his people in the face of Ammonite aggression. Scene one begins with an external threat altering an internal division. Initiative comes from the elders of Gilead whose vacuous military establishment has left them no choice but to seek out the illegitimate one to save them. These elders "went to bring Jephthah from the land of Tob" (11:5b, RSV).[14] At first, they offer him only temporary authority during the forthcoming fight with the Ammonites. "Come and be our leader (*qāṣîn*) . . . ," they implore (11:6, RSV).[15] But Jephthah challenges the elders with questions recalling his harsh treatment at their hands (11:7).[16] Though they deny these accusations, desperation impels them to offer him permanent authority:

> Now we have turned to you
>   that you may go with us
>   and fight the children of Ammon;
>   that you may be for us head (*lĕrōš*)
>   of all the inhabitants of Gilead.
>   (11:8, RSV*)[17]

Amazingly, the elders award this enormous power to Jephthah without even specifying that he must win the battle.

Their revised offer brings Jephthah to the point of bargaining:

> If you ('attem) cause me ('ôtî) to return
> to fight the children of Ammon
> and (if) Yahweh gives them to me,
> then I ('ānōkî) shall be
> over you (lākem) head (lĕrōš).
>
> (11:9)[18]

The bargaining is shrewd. By appealing conditionally to Yahweh, Jephthah decreases further the power of the elders while enhancing his own authority. What they have just offered, he proposes to earn on the battlefield, if the Lord so wills. Then, once the condition is fulfilled and the battle won, Jephthah alone will claim permanent power without reference to Yahweh. According to the words here, the deity who is useful in the bargaining process has no part in the aftermath of victory. And so the divine enters the story obliquely, neither speaking nor acting nor being addressed directly. Such religious language will in time exacerbate the terror and perplexity of all that happens. Meanwhile, in their reply to Jephthah, the elders acquiesce completely to his bargain. Faced with an external threat, Gilead has resolved its internal conflicts. A public danger has settled a private crisis. With Jephthah as their "head and leader" (11:11), the children of Israel are ready to confront the children of Ammon.[19]

The initial confrontation is an exercise in diplomacy. On two separate occasions the enemies talk, with the narrator providing information and commentary (11:12–13, 14–28). Emissaries take Jephthah's words to the unnamed king of the Ammonites: "What is at issue between us that you have come to fight against my land?" (11:12).[20] The answer is uncompromising. To the charge that the Ammonites have come "to fight against *my land*," the king counters that "Israel on coming from Egypt took away *my land*" (11:13). In a territorial dispute, the king seeks restoration. A second time Jephthah sends messengers to the monarch. They make a lengthy speech in the style of a prophetic lawsuit where the standard formula, "Thus says the Lord," becomes instead, "Thus says Jephthah" (11:5).[21] "But the king of the Ammonites would not heed the words of Jephthah which he sent to him" (11:28, RSV*).[22] This conclusion to scene one leads to the battle that provides the occasion for our story.

SCENE TWO IN CONTEXT

A. *Episode One: Joining the Battle, 11:29–33.* Though Jephthah, the elders of Gilead, and the narrator have all invoked the Lord, at no point thus far has the deity actually intervened. Striking, then, is the narrative report that commences episode one of scene two: "Then the spirit of Yahweh came upon Jephthah" (11:29). The formulaic speech clearly establishes divine sanction for the events that follow and predicts their successful resolution.[23] But Jephthah himself does not evince the assurance that the spirit of Yahweh ought to give. Rather than acting with conviction and courage, he responds with doubt and demand. At the very center (11:30–31) of the battle episode, he disrupts the narration (11:29, 32–33) to make yet another bargain. So serious are his words that the storyteller designates them a vow. "Now Jephthah vowed a vow to Yahweh" (11:30a).[24]

Unlike his earlier scheme addressed to the elders of Gilead (11:9), this vow beseeches God directly, with pressuring language: "If you will *really* give . . . ," begins Jephthah. The use of the infinitive absolute in Hebrew (*nātôn*, translated here adverbially) may suggest that Jephthah is pushing the bargaining mode of discourse to its limit. The chosen savior, endowed with the spirit of Yahweh, is nevertheless unsure of divine help and insecure about his future among those who had once rejected him. Therefore, he implores the deity, "If you will *really* give the Ammonites into my hand. . . ." The intensity of this protasis leads to a resolute apodosis: "Then whatsoever comes forth from the doors of my house to meet me upon my return in victory from the Ammonites shall belong to Yahweh; I will offer it as a burnt offering" (11:30). In moving from condition to outcome, Jephthah switches from direct address to a third-person reference for the deity: "Whatsoever comes forth . . . shall belong to Yahweh." Though this third person reference corresponds to usages of the divine name elsewhere in the story,[25] its appearance in the apodosis of this sentence is special. Unlike Jephthah's earlier bargain, this vow implicates the Lord in the outcome of the condition. Beyond doubt, the sacrifice will be made *to Yahweh.*[26]

The nature of the sacrifice is, however, as unclear as it is emphatic.

Literally, the words read, "the comer-forth who comes forth," a compound expression of emphasis that is difficult to render in English. Moreover, the masculine gender of these terms is a standard grammatical usage that by itself does not identify either species or sex. A certain vagueness lurks in these words of Jephthah, and we do well to let it be. Did he intend a human sacrifice, male or female? A servant perhaps? Or an animal?[27] The story fails to clarify here the precise meaning of his words; we shall know it by the fruits.

In linking his private life with a public crisis, the savior figure has spoken on his own, for neither Yahweh nor the people of Gilead require the vow. Furthermore, his speech has disrupted the flow of the narrated discourse. It has broken in at the very center to press for divine help that ironically is already Jephthah's through the spirit of Yahweh. The making of the vow is an act of unfaithfulness. Jephthah desires to bind God rather than embrace the gift of the spirit. What comes to him freely, he seeks to earn and manipulate. The meaning of his words is doubt, not faith; it is control, not courage. To such a vow the deity makes no reply.

"So Jephthah passed over to the Ammonites to fight against them" (11:32a).[28] As we would expect, since the spirit of Yahweh is upon him, the outcome is victory. In reporting the result, the narrator borrows language from the vow itself. "If you will really give the Ammonites into my hand," Jephthah had implored. Now we read, "Yahweh gave them into his hand" (11:32b). Those words that earlier broke the narration here become part of it. Artistically, this reference to Yahweh at the end of the scene balances the phrase "spirit of Yahweh" at the beginning; yet the two statements are in tension. In the first, the spirit of Yahweh is a gift to Jephthah that guarantees the desired outcome but is not subject to it. By contrast, the second statement, "Yahweh gave them into his hand," using the vocabulary of the vow, violates the language of unqualified gift. In other words, the working out of the vow to Yahweh has replaced the free bounty of the spirit of the Lord. Jephthah has gotten what he wanted in the way he wanted it, but he does not understand that to win is to lose. By appropriating Jephthah's speech, the storyteller heightens the efficacy of the vow, forecasts its continuing power, *and* alters the theological stance of the story.

After making this theological shift, the narrator supplies details of the victory (11:33). How great was the slaughter; how decisive the defeat! Even the syntax of the sentences discloses the changed status of the Ammonites. Whereas in earlier reports they were aggressors (10:17; 11:4, 5), in this and subsequent episodes they become objects acted upon (11:32, 33) or talked about (11:36; 12:1–3). Those who "made war against Israel" (11:4) are now "subdued before the people of Israel" (11:33). Warfare has accomplished what words failed to do. It has resolved the opposition between Israel and Ammon that initiated the story.

B. *Episode Two: Reaping the Victory, 11:34–39b.* Yet the scene is not finished. Slaughter in episode one begets sacrifice in episode two. As the particular focus of our study, this latter episode merits close analysis. A symmetrical arrangement characterizes its form and content. At the same time, differences in the length of the parts skew the symmetry to vary the meanings.[29] The unit opens (11:34–35a) and closes (11:38b–39b) with narrated discourse. It surrounds direct discourse (11:35b–38a). In each section of the narrated discourse, actions by Jephthah surround descriptions of his daughter. Similarly, the direct discourse consists of two speeches by the father (11:35b and 11:38a) surrounding two speeches by the daughter (11:36 and 11:37). Design and content show that he confines her, even unto death:

a *Narrated discourse: Jephthah confines his daughter.*

Now Jephthah came to Mizpah to his home.

> Just at that very moment his daughter came forth
> to meet him with timbrels and dances.
> She was his one and only child;
> besides her he had neither son nor daughter.

Upon seeing her, he rent his clothes.

b *Direct discourse: The father speaks.*

And he said:

> "Ah, my daughter!
> You have brought me low;
> You have become my calamity.
> I have opened my mouth to Yahweh
> and I cannot turn back."

c *Direct discourse: The daughter speaks.*

And she said to him:

> "My father,
> You have opened your mouth to Yahweh;
> do to me according to what goes forth
> from your mouth,
> since Yahweh has done to you deliverance
> from your enemies, from the Ammonites."

c' *Direct discourse: The daughter speaks.*

And she said to her father:

> "Let this thing be done for me:
> Let me alone for two months
> that I may go and wander upon the hills
> and lament my virginity—
> I and my female friends."

b' *Direct discourse: The father speaks.*

And he said:

> "Go."

a' *Narrated discourse: Jephthah confines his daughter unto death.*

So he sent her away for two months.

> She went, she and her female friends,
> and she lamented her virginity upon the hills.
> At the end of two months, she returned to her father.

And he did to her his vow which he had vowed.

(11:34–39b, RSV*)

(a) Episode two reaps the victory that Jephthah has sought; his vow must be redeemed. Appropriately, the location is Mizpah, the site of both Israel's encampment against the Ammonites and Jephthah's words before the Lord (11:11; cf. 11:29–31). Though once he dwelt in the land of Tob, the outcast-turned-deliverer is now established in the city of Gilead. His victory over the Ammonites leads him predictably to the threshold of his own home: "Jephthah came to Mizpah, to his home" (11:34a). This introductory statement recalls Jephthah's vow, and so it evokes anticipation, even anxiety. What will meet him? The storyteller underscores the answer with the use of the emphatic Hebrew word *hinnēh*, usually rendered "behold," followed directly by the familial subject, "his-daughter."[30] We may translate it, "Just at that very moment his daughter. . . ."[31] The two Hebrew words alone are chilling harbingers of the terror that is to unfold. The next words confirm the horror because they come directly from the vow of Jephthah. He had promised, "Whatsoever comes forth (*yṣ'*) . . . to meet (*qr'*) me" (11:31). Now we are told, "Just at that very moment his daughter came forth (*yṣ'*) to meet (*qr'*) him" (11:34b). The ambiguity of Jephthah's vow disappears. His daughter is his sacrifice; she must die for his unfaithfulness. If Jephthah suffered for the sins of his parents, how much more shall this child bear because of the machinations of her father. Unfaithfulness reaches into the third generation to bring forth a despicable fruit. "Is there no balm in Gilead?" (Jer. 8:22).

"Just at that very moment his daughter came forth to meet him." Immediately we know, but she does not. "With music (*tuppîm*) and dancing (*mĕḥōlôt*)," she comes forth to celebrate her father's victory. She moves freely, unaware that her joyful initiative seals her death. To those acquainted with the traditions of her people, her appearance and activity are no surprise. Long ago, after Yahweh brought back the water of the sea upon Pharaoh, his horses, and his horsemen, Miriam, the prophet, "took a timbrel in her hand; and all the women went out (*yṣ'*) after her with music (*tuppîm*) and dancing (*mĕḥōlôt*). And Miriam sang to them:

> Sing unto Yahweh, glorious deity!
> The horse and the rider God has hurled into the sea."
> (Exod. 15:19–21)

And centuries later, "when David returned from slaying the Philistines, the women came out (*yṣ'*) of all the cities of Israel, singing and dancing (*mĕḥōlôt*) to meet (*qr'*) King Saul with timbrels (*tuppîm*), with songs of joy and instruments of music. And the women sang to one another as they made merry:

> Saul has slain his thousands,
> and David his ten thousands."
> (1 Sam. 18:6–7)

To such an ancient and noble company of women belongs the daughter of Jephthah, coming out (*yṣ'*) "with timbrels and dances" to meet (qr') her victorious father. Unlike them, she comes alone, and no words of a song appear on her lips. The difference accents the terrible irony of an otherwise typical and joyful occasion. Moreover, the narrator stresses the isolation of the child *and* the dilemma of the parent through an extraordinary accumulation of expressions: "She was his one and only child;[32] besides her he had neither son nor daughter" (11:34c).

Once before in the traditions of Israel such language occurred with comparable poignancy. On that occasion God spoke to a mighty warrior who had been victorious in battle (Gen. 14:13–24).[33] "Abraham, . . . take your son, your only one (*yĕḥîdĕkā*), whom you love, Isaac . . . and offer him as a burnt offering . . ." (Gen. 22:2; cf. 22:12, 16).[34] That utterance by God began a divine test of faithfulness, but our description by the narrator belongs to a human vow of unfaithfulness about which God has kept silent. Jephthah is not Abraham; distrust, not faith, has singled out his one and only child. Furthermore, the son of promise had a name: Isaac. He also had a respectable family lineage: a mother named Sarai (Gen. 11:29) and a grandfather named Terah (Gen. 11:27). By contrast, the daughter of the mighty warrior Jephthah is nameless. Her father is of illegitimate birth; her mother is never mentioned; her grandmother was a harlot; and her grandfather cannot be identified. So the girl emerges as an isolated figure in the traditions of Israel as well as in this particular story. "She was his one and only child; besides her he had neither son nor daughter." If the narrator's description singles her out for pity, nevertheless, at the same time, it evokes sympathy for Jephthah whose own vow threatens to destroy his most precious possession. Father and daughter are held together in the ambiguity of tragedy.

In coming forth from the house to meet the victorious warrior, the daughter fulfills the language of her father's vow. The horror of the situation is clear to the audience before the characters themselves confront it. When he does see her, Jephthah rents his clothes (11:35a). It is a gesture of despair, grief, and mourning[35]—but for whom? What the narrated words hint, the direct discourse boldly proclaims. Jephthah mourns for himself, not for his daughter.

(b) A cry of anguish leaves his lips, "Ah,[36] my daughter!" to be followed, however, by strong words of accusation: "You have brought me low (*kr*ᶜ); you (*'att*) have become my calamity (ᶜ*kr*; 11:35b).³⁷ At the beginning of the first clause in Hebrew, the Hiphil infinitive absolute (*hakrēaᶜ*) stresses the devastating deed of the daughter;³⁸ at the beginning of the second clause, the independent pronoun *you* further accents her as the cause of the calamity;³⁹ and between these two clauses a wordplay on the verb *bring low* and the noun *calamity* underscores again the censure placed on her. All together five Hebrew words intensify the condemnation of the child by her father. Some ancient versions include still a third clause: "You have become a stumbling block for me."⁴⁰ Repeatedly, Jephthah's language triumphs; blame overwhelms the victim. At the moment of recognition and disclosure, Jephthah thinks of himself and indicts his daughter for the predicament. "I" (*'ānōkî*), he continues emphatically, "have opened my mouth to Yahweh, and I cannot turn back" (11:35c).

Faithfulness to an unfaithful vow has condemned its victim; father and daughter are split apart in deed and destiny. Though in anguish he calls her "my daughter," he offers her neither solace nor release. His words diverge from the compassion of Abraham, who evasively yet faithfully assured Isaac, "God will provide himself the lamb for a burnt offering, my son" (Gen. 22:8). Unlike the father Abraham, Jephthah fails to evoke the freedom of the deity to avert disaster. Nor does he wish to die instead of his child, as did the father David (2 Sam. 19:1).⁴¹ Although his daughter has served him devotedly with music and dance, Jephthah bewails the calamity that she brings upon him. And throughout it all God says nothing.

(c) With courage and determination the daughter answers her father. Though she is not told the specific content of his vow,⁴² the inevitability of his words is sufficient. She does not seek to deny or defy them, nor does she show anger or depression. No sentiment of self-pity passes her lips; instead, she feels for her father the compassion that he has not extended to her. "She said to him, 'My father.'" Once Isaac uttered the same word of intimacy (Gen. 22:7), but how different is that language now. Unlike Isaac, this child knows what the father must do, and yet she embraces him with speech. How different also is her address from her father's. "My daughter" yielded recrimination and self-concern; "my father" brings justification and courage. Both responses testify, however, to the inviolability of the vow spoken to the deity (cf. Num. 30:3; Deut. 23:22–24).

"I have opened my mouth to Yahweh," said Jephthah, "and I cannot turn back." The daughter's reply echoes that understanding:

> You have opened your mouth to Yahweh;
> do to me according to what goes forth from your mouth,
>   since Yahweh has done to you deliverance
>   from your enemies, from the Ammonites.
>
>   (11:36)[43]

The word that has gone forth (*yṣ'*) from his mouth (11:36) has become the daughter who has gone forth (*yṣ'*) from his house (11:34). To her he must do (*'śh*) what he has declared to the Lord, because the Lord has done (*'śh*) for him what he asked. The young woman understands well. She knows that "death and life are in the power of the tongue" (Prov. 18:21). Hence, she holds her father to his vow; she does not pray that this cup pass from her.

(c') Nevertheless, hers is not quiet acquiescence. Within the limits of the inevitable she takes charge to bargain for herself. The victim assumes responsibility, not for blame but for integrity. Thus the narrator reports her second speech: "And she said to her father" (11:37a). This time the storyteller, not the daughter, uses the paternal vocabulary. The difference is distance. Having already embraced her father with words, the child steps back from the one who is to be her executioner. Her request makes clear this separation: "Let this thing (*dābār*) be done for me," she begins (11:37b, RSV). The verb and its prepositional object play upon her earlier speech. "Do (*'śh*) to me (*lî*)," she had said, because the Lord "has done (*'śh*) to you (*lĕkā*)." First, however, "Let this thing be done (*'śh*) for me (*lî*):

> Let me alone for two months
>   that I may go and wander[44] upon the hills
>   and lament my virginity—
> I and my female friends."
>
>   (11:37c)

The request is for a respite, a time and place apart from her father and his vow. That time is to be filled with lamentation, not for death, but for unfulfilled life.

To be sure, death belongs to life: "We must all die; we are like water spilt on the ground, which cannot be gathered up again" (2 Sam. 14:14). Yet this particular death defies all the categories of the natural and the expected.[45] First, it is premature; life ends before its potential has unfolded. If King Hezekiah could weep bitterly that "in the noontide" of his days he must depart (Isa. 38:3, 10), how much more this child must lament in the morning of her life. Second, her death is to be violent. Death by fire is bitter death, and more bitter still when its author is her very own father. Third, her death will leave no heirs because she is a virgin. What alone designated fulfillment for every Hebrew woman, the bearing of children, will never be hers to know (cf. 1 Sam. 1:1–20). Truly, with no child to succeed her, she may be numbered among the unremembered, those "who have perished as though they had not lived" (Sirach 44:9). Premature, violent, without an heir: all the marks of unnatural death befall this young woman, and she is not even spared the knowledge of them. Hers is premeditated death, a sentence of murder passed upon an innocent victim because of the faithless vow uttered by her foolish father. These conditions shroud the request she makes of him: "that I may go and wander upon the hills and lament my virginity."

The closing words of her speech introduce a new dimension to the story. Thus far emphasis has fallen upon her isolation. She is "the one and only child"; by herself she greets her father with music and dances; and she requests that he let her alone for two months. But then she adds, "I (*'ānōkî*) and my female friends." At the time of deepest sorrow, the last days of her life, the girl reaches out to other women. She chooses them to go with her to wander upon the hills and lament her virginity. In communion with her own kind, she transcends the distance between daughter and father. After this reference to female friends, she speaks no more. Within the limits of the inevitable she has shaped meaning for herself.

(b', a') Simply and succinctly the father grants the request. "Go," he says—his last word in the story (11:38a). From here on, only the narrator speaks. Adopting the daughter's speech pattern, the storyteller reports the fulfillment of her plan: "So he sent her away for two months. She went, she and her female friends, and she lamented her virginity upon the hills" (11:38). In the company of other women who acknowledge her tragedy, she is neither alone nor isolated. She spends the last days of her life as she has requested.

At the end of two months, the appointed time, the daughter returns to the father (11:39a). Quickly, without passing judgment, the narrator tells the deed: "He did to her his vow which he had vowed" (11:39b). How different is this story from Abraham's sacrifice of Isaac, where detail heaped upon detail slows down the narrative to build suspense for the climactic moment.

> When they came to the place of which God had told him,
> Abraham built an altar there and laid the wood in order,
> and bound Isaac his son, and laid him on the altar,
>   upon the wood.
> Then Abraham put forth his hand and took the knife
>   to slay his son.
>   (Gen. 22:9–10, RSV)

That suspense is bearable because Isaac is to be spared. At the last moment, the angel of the Lord negates the divine imperative, "Kill your child," by another command, "Do not lay your hand on the lad or do anything to him" (Gen. 22:12a, RSV). But in the story of the daughter of Jephthah, no angel intervenes to save the child. The father carries out the human vow precisely as he spoke it; neither God nor man nor woman negates it. Accordingly, the narrator spares us the suspense and agony of details; the despicable outcome is sufficient unto itself. Five Hebrew words tell the tale: "And-he-did to-her his-vow which he-had-vowed" (11:39c). Though the son was saved, the daughter is slain.[46] Surely, "the victory that day was turned into mourning" (2 Sam. 19:2, RSV).

The verb *do* has now completed its life in this episode. "*Do* to me," she had said, "according to what goes forth from your mouth, since Yahweh *has done* to you deliverance" (11:36). Thus, "he *did* to her his vow which he had vowed" (11:39b). Further, the vocabulary of the vow returns us to the beginning of the entire scene (11:30), thereby interlocking public and private crises in a composition of circularity.[47] A vow led to victory; victory produced a vic-

n died by violence; violence has, in turn, fulfilled the
ginning to end, this faithless and foolish vow has been
controls both father and daughter, though in different
ways. Moreover, in its presence even the deity to whom it was
addressed remains silent.[48] Under the power of the vow, the daughter has breathed her last. My God, my God, why hast thou forsaken
her?[49]

C. *Positing a Postscript, 11:39c–40*. Death and silence are not, however, the final words of the story. In fact, a narrative postscript shifts
the meaning from vow to victim; from the father who survives to
the daughter who, dying prematurely and violently, has no child to
keep her name in remembrance (cf. 2 Sam. 18:18). At the beginning
of the postscript, the narrator reemphasizes her barrenness. "Now
she had not known a man" (11:38c). The next three words have been
translated almost unanimously through the ages as, "and it became
a custom in Israel" (11:39d). The verb in the clause is a feminine
singular form of *be* or *become*. Since Hebrew has no neuter gender,
such feminine forms may carry a neuter meaning[50] so that the traditional reading, "it became," is certainly legitimate—but it may
not be perceptive. Indeed, grammar, content, and context provide
compelling reasons for departing from this translation. After all, the
preceding clause has *she* as the subject of its verb: "Now she had
not known a man." An independent feminine pronoun (*hi'*) accents
the subject. Similarly, the feminine grammatical gender of the verb
become may refer to the daughter herself.[51] Further, the term that
is usually designated *custom* (*ḥōq*) can also mean *tradition*.[52] The
resulting translation would be, "She became a tradition in Israel."

In other words, the postscript reports an extraordinary development. Whereas the female who has never known a man is typically
numbered among the unremembered, in the case of the daughter of
Jephthah the usual does not happen. "Although *she* had not known
a man, nevertheless *she* became a tradition in Israel." In a dramatic
way this sentence alters, though it does not eliminate, the finality
of Jephthah's faithless vow. The alteration comes through the faithfulness of the women of Israel, as the next line explains. "From
year to year the daughters of Israel went to mourn for the daughter
of Jephthah the Gileadite, four days in the year" (11:40).[53] The un-

named virgin child becomes a tradition in Israel because the women with whom she chose to spend her last days have not let her pass into oblivion. They have established a testimony: activities of mourning reiterated yearly in a special place.[54] This they have done in remembrance of her (cf. 1 Cor. 11:24–25). The narrative postscript, then, shifts the focus of the story from vow to victim, from death to life, from oblivion to remembrance. Remarkably, this saga of faithlessness and sacrifice mitigates, though it does not dispel, its own tragedy through the mourning of women.

RESPONSES TO THE STORY

From the Scriptures. "Is it nothing to you, all you who pass by?" (Lam. 1:12a, RSV). Sadly, the scriptures of faith have failed to perceive and interpret the nuances of this story. Throughout centuries patriarchal hermeneutics has forgotten the daughter of Jephthah but remembered her father, indeed exalted him. The earliest evidence is in the conclusion of the Jephthah cycle of stories. It shifts attention from the private crisis of sacrifice to a public confrontation between tribes (12:1–7).[55] Challenged by armed Ephraimites, Jephthah leads the Gileadites to a resounding victory. The mighty warrior prevails uncensured; the violence that he perpetrated upon his only daughter stalks him not at all.[56] In the end he dies a natural death and receives an epitaph fit for an exemplary judge (12:7).[57] Moreover, his military victories enhance his name in the years to come. Specifically, the prophet Samuel proclaims to Israel that "Yahweh sent . . . Jephthah . . . and delivered you out of the hand of your enemies . . ." (1 Sam. 12:11, RSV).

What the Old Testament begins, the Apocrypha continues. In Sirach's litany of praise for famous men, we infer that Jephthah has a place among

> The judges also, with their respective names,
>   those whose hearts did not fall into idolatry
> and who did not turn away from the Lord—
>   may their memory be blessed!
> May their bones revive from where they lie,
>   and may the name of those who have been honored
>   live again in their sons![58]
>
> (Sirach 46:11–12, RSV)

What the Apocrypha continues,[59] the New Testament concludes triumphantly. In the Epistle to the Hebrews, Jephthah is explicitly named as one "who *through faith* conquered kingdoms, enforced justice, . . . escaped the edge of the sword, won strength out of weakness, became mighty in war, put foreign armies to flight" (Heb. 11:32–34, RSV*). Jephthah is praised; his daughter forgotten. Unfaith becomes faith. Thus has scripture violated the ancient story, and yet that story endures to this day for us to recover and appropriate.

From the Readers. Like the daughters of Israel, we remember and mourn the daughter of Jephthah the Gileadite. In her death we are all diminished; by our memory she is forever hallowed. Though not a "survivor," she becomes an unmistakable symbol for all the courageous daughters of faithless fathers. Her story, brief as it is, evokes the imagination, calling forth a reader's response.[60] Surely words of lament are a seemly offering, for did not the daughters of Israel mourn the daughter of Jephthah every year? Now the biblical tradition itself provides both a model and foil for just such an offering: the lament of David for Saul and Jonathan, for a father and son who died prematurely in the violence of battle (2 Sam. 1:19–27). Overcome by grief, David cried:

> Thy glory, O Israel, is slain upon thy high places!
>   How are the mighty fallen!
>   (2 Sam. 1:19, RSV)

Using these haunting words as point and counterpoint, let us in the spirit of the daughters of Israel remember and mourn the daughter of Jephthah:

> Thy daughter, O Israel, is slain upon thy high places!
>   How are the powerless fallen!
> Tell it in Ammon,
>   publish it in the streets of Rabbah;
> for the daughters of the Ammonites will not rejoice;
>   the daughters of the enemies will not exult.
>
> Tell it also in Gilead,
>   publish it in the streets of Mizpah;
> for the sons of Israel do forget,
>   the sons of the covenant remember not at all.

Ye valleys of Gilead,
   let there be no dew or rain upon you,
   nor upsurging of the deep,
for there the innocence of the powerless was defiled,
   the only daughter of the mighty was offered up.

From the tyranny of the vow,
   from the blood of the sacrifice,
the unnamed child turned not back,
   the courage of the daughter turned not away.

Daughter of Jephthah, beloved and lovely!
   In life and in death a virgin child,
Greeting her father with music and dances,
   facing his blame with clarity and strength.

Ye daughters of Israel, weep for your sister,
   who suffered the betrayal of her foolish father,
   who turned to you for solace and love.

How are the powerless fallen
   in the midst of the victory!

The daughter of Jephthah lies slain upon thy high places.
I weep for you, my little sister.
Very poignant is your story to me;
   your courage to me is wonderful,
   surpassing the courage of men.

How are the powerless fallen,
   a terrible sacrifice to a faithless vow!

NOTES

1. Anthropologists teach that the word *tribe* should be used with caution. See, e.g., Morton H. Fried, *The Notion of Tribe* (Menlo Park, Calif.: Cummings Publishing Co., 1975); J. W. Rogerson, *Anthropology and the Old Testament* (Atlanta: John Knox Press, 1979), pp. 86–101. For sociological studies of the tribes of ancient Israel, see George E. Mendenhall, *The Tenth Generation* (Baltimore: Johns Hopkins University Press, 1973), especially pp. 1–31, 174–97; Norman K. Gottwald, *The Tribes of Yahweh* (Maryknoll, N.Y.: Orbis Books, 1979), *passim* and especially pp. 294–98. Standard historical treatments of the period of the judges include A. D. H. Mayes, "The Period of the Judges and the Rise of the Monarchy," in *Israelite and Judean History*, ed. John H. Hayes and J. Maxwell Miller, OTL (Philadelphia: Westminster Press, 1977), especially pp. 285–93, 297–322; A. D. H. Mayes, *Israel in the Period of the Judges* (Naperville, Ill.: Alec R. Allenson, 1974); John Bright, *A History of Israel* (Philadelphia: Westminster Press, 1972),

pp. 140–75; Manfred Weippert, *The Settlement of the Israelite Tribes in Palestine* (Naperville, Ill.: Alec R. Allenson, 1971); John L. McKenzie, S.J., *The World of the Judges* (Englewood Cliffs, N.J.: Prentice-Hall, 1966), especially pp. 144–50.

2. In this chapter the word *saga* means story.

3. For a form-critical and traditio-historical study of the Jephthah cycle, see Wolfgang Richter, "Die Überlieferungen um Jephtah. Ri. 10,17–12,6," *Biblica* 47 (1966): 485–556. For a literary study, see Robert Polzin, *Moses and the Deuteronomist* (New York: Seabury Press, 1980), pp. 176–81.

4. Wherever they are not identified in this essay, chapter and verse citations come from the book of Judges.

5. The major divisions of the Jephthah cycle are as follows:
Theological Preface (10:6–16)
A. Introduction: The Juxtaposition of Crises (10:17—11:3)
   1. Public crisis: enmity between nations (10:17–18)
   2. Private crisis: enmity between brothers (11:1–3)
B. Scene One: Decision and Discord (11:4–28)
   1. Resolution: the private crisis within Israel (11:4–11)
   2. Conflict: the public crisis between Ammon and Israel (11:12–28)
C. Scene Two: Slaughter and Sacrifice, with a postscript (11:29–40)
   1. Resolution: the public slaughter of Ammon by Israel (11:29–33)
   2. Conflict: the private sacrifice of his daughter by Jephthah (11:34–39b)
   3. A postscript *in memoriam* (11:39c–40)
D. Conclusion: The Aftermath of Conflict and Death (12:1–7)
   1. Intertribal conflict: Ephraim versus Gilead (12:1–6)
     a. Words of accusation (12:1–3)
     b. Words of death (12:4–6)
   2. The death of Jephthah (12:7)

6. On Ammonite history and civilization, see G. M. Landes, "Ammon, Ammonites," *IDB* 1, pp. 108–14, and S. H. Horn, "Ammon, Ammonites," *IDBS*, p. 20.

7. On the composition of the book of Judges, specifically the Deuteronomic edition, see Robert G. Boling, *Judges*, Anchor Bible (New York: Doubleday & Co., 1975), especially pp. 34–38, 193.

8. The question asked in 10:18 convicts the questioners, for the leaders are refusing to lead. So great is their desire to shift responsibility that they promise to make a new leader "head (*rōš*) over all the inhabitants of Gilead." On the title *head*, see below.

9. See Boling, *Judges*, p. 197.

10. See C. F. Burney, *The Book of Judges* (New York: KTAV Publishing House, 1970), p. 308; Boling, *Judges*, p. 197.

11. For a comparison of the expulsion of Jephthah with the sending away of Ishmael, see Thomas L. Thompson, *The Historicity of the Patriarchal Narratives* (Berlin: Walter de Gruyter, 1974), p. 258.

12. Tob was a nearby Syrian town that upon occasion showed sympathy to the Ammonites; see 2 Sam. 10:6, 8.

13. Thus this section (11:1–3) closes with an emphatic pronoun that matches the beginning: "*He* was the son of a prostitute . . . worthless fellows went raiding with *him*."

14. Their action is answered at the end of the episode where the subject and object of the verb *go* (*hlk*) reverse: ". . . the elders of Gilead went to bring Jephthah from the land of Tob" (11:5). "So Jephthah went with the elders of Gilead" (11:11). Between these corresponding narrative statements lies the direct discourse of the elders and the outcast, negotiations that succeed in turning the power structure upside down: object becomes subject.

15. The use of the term *leader* (*qāṣîn*) contrasts with the word head (*rōš*) in 10:18. This switch introduces a tension that is not finally resolved until 11:11.

16. In his first question, which concerns the past (11:7b), Jephthah begins with the emphatic pronouns *you* ('*attem*) and *me* ('*ôtî*); they oppose each other by the intervention of the verb *hate* (*śn'*). In the second question, which concerns the present (11:7c), he describes himself once again as the object of the elders' action and ends the sentence with the pronoun *you* (*lākem*). Thus the form and content of these interrogative utterances depict interpersonal captivity: The *you* of the elders surrounds (i.e., seeks to control) the *me* of Jephthah.

17. Note that the pronouns in 11:8 begin to shift power to Jephthah. He becomes subject; the elders become objects. Note also that the elders switch their offer from *leader* (11:6) to *head* (cf. 10:18). Whereas the former title was to be given before the battle, the latter is to be awarded afterward (though victory itself is not specified). This inversion may suggest that the title *head* denotes a permanent tribal chief, and *leader*, a temporary military position; see Boling, *Judges*, p. 198; McKenzie, *The World of the Judges*, pp. 145–46.

18. Note the play on the verb (*re*)*turn* (*šûb*) in 11:8, 9. Observe also in 11:9a the use of the emphatic pronouns *you* and *me*, which occur side by side in Hebrew with no intervening verb (cf. note 16 above). In other words, opposition ceases between the *you* of the elders and the *me* of Jephthah. Further, in the apodosis of this conditional sentence (11:9c), Jephthah prevails over the elders: his *I* ('*ānōkî*) as head (*lĕrōš*) surrounds the *you* (*lākem*) of the elders (cf. 11:7).

19. In bringing together the titles *head* and *leader*, the narrator alters understandings that developed earlier in the direct discourses. Here the order of the titles is reversed from their appearance in 11:6, 8; moreover, both are conferred before victory, indeed before battle, thereby dispensing with Jephthah's own condition (11:9). Any tension or ambiguity concerning the status of Jephthah disappears. Combined, these two titles legitimate absolutely the power of the illegitimate one. Further, the elders have already promised to do "according to the word (*dbr*) of Jephthah" (11:10). Now Jephthah gives "all his words" (*dbr*) the character of a sacred oath by speaking (*dbr*) them before Yahweh at Mizpah (11:11), the site where Israel was encamped against the Ammonites (10:17). These two references to Mizpah suggest an *inclusio* whereby a public crisis has resolved an internal conflict. The question first asked at Mizpah (10:17–18) is answered by

Jephthah's arrival there (11:11). What a change has been wrought at Mizpah! On Jephthah as deliverer (*Retter*) in the crisis and ruler (*Richter*) after the battle, see Hartmut N. Rösel, "Jephthah und das Problem der Richter," *Biblica* 61 (1980): 251–55.

20. The sharpness of the interrogative sentence echoes Jephthah's earlier questions to the elders of Gilead, whom he then considered to be his enemies (11:7). For a form-critical study of this entire section, see Claus Westermann, *Basic Forms of Prophetic Speech* (Philadelphia: Westminster Press, 1967), pp. 111–15.

21. For exegetical details, see Boling, *Judges*, pp. 200–205 and the bibliography cited there. In light of our interests, note the use of the interrogative sentences by Jephthah in 11:23b–26. Also observe in 11:27a the use of emphatic pronouns separated by verbs that place in opposition the two peoples: "*I* ('*ānōkî*) have not sinned against you (*lāk*), but *you* ('*attāh*) have done *me* ('*ittî*) evil to fight against me (*bî*)"; cf. 11:7, 9.

22. The phrase, "words of Jephthah," plays upon the narrative ending of the preceding episode (11:11). Though the words (*dbr*) to the king have been ineffectual, the words (*dbr*) spoken before Yahweh will not return empty.

23. See Boling, *Judges*, p. 207. *Mutatis mutandis*, cf., e.g., Judg. 3:10; 6:34; 14:6, 19; 1 Sam. 11:6.

24. On the nature of a vow, see G. Henton Davies, "Vows," *IDB* 4, pp. 792–93; J. Pedersen, *Israel*, III–IV (London: Oxford University Press, 1963), pp. 322–30. Cf. Simon B. Parker, "The Vow in Ugaritic and Israelite Narrative Literature," *Ugarit-Forschungen* 11 (1979): 693–700, especially 696–97.

25. E.g., Judg. 11:9–11, 21, 23, 24, 27, 29.

26. Attempts to make the vow non-Yahwistic are futile: e.g., John H. Otwell, *And Sarah Laughed* (Philadelphia: Westminster Press, 1977), pp. 70–71. See Alberto Ravinell Whitney Green, *The Role of Human Sacrifice in the Ancient Near East* (Missoula, Mont.: Scholars Press, 1975), pp. 161–63; A. van Hoonacker, "La voeu de Jephté," *Le Muséon* 11 (Louvain, 1892): 448–69; 12 (1893): 59–80. Cf. Num. 21:2–3, where, in the context of holy war, Israel "vowed a vow to Yahweh and said, 'If you will really give this people into my hand, then I will utterly destroy their cities.'" Note the verbal and formal similarities to Jephthah's vow but also the striking difference in the content of the two apodoses. Though Israel vowed to destroy the enemy after victory, Jephthah vows to sacrifice from his own house.

27. See Boling, *Judges*, pp. 208–9, who proposes animal sacrifice; cf. Gen. 22:13. *Contra* George F. Moore, *A Critical and Exegetical Commentary on Judges*, ICC (New York: Charles Scribner's Sons, 1910), p. 299, who wrote, "That a human victim is intended is, in fact, as plain as words can make it"; similarly, Burney, *Judges*, pp. 319–20. Pedersen, *Israel*, p. 326; Green, *The Role of Human Sacrifice in the Ancient Near East*, p. 162. On the possibility of a servant, see John Dominic Crossan, "Judges," in *The Jerome Biblical Commentary*, vol. I, ed. Raymond E. Brown, S.S. et al. (Englewood Cliffs, N.J.: Prentice-Hall, 1968), p. 158.

28. The verb *pass over* (*ʿbr*), with Jephthah as its subject, joins the beginning (11:29, where it occurs three times) and the end (11:32–33) of this literary unit.

29. Cf. the arrangement of Hans-Winfried Jüngling, *Richter 19—Ein Plädoyer für das Königtum* (Rome: Biblical Institute Press, 1981), pp. 165–67. Cf. also the arrangement of 11:5–11; see note 14 above. *Contra* Richter ("Die Überlieferungen um Jephtah," pp. 503–17), I find no "tension" between 11:34–36 and 11:37–40, though I designate 11:39c–40 as the postscript; see below.

30. Cf. the usual order of a Hebrew sentence in which verb precedes subject.

31. On translations of *hinnēh*, see chapter 3, note 20 above.

32. The emphasis is truly extraordinary, literally reading, "only (*raq*) she (*hî*'), an only one (*yĕhîdāh*)." The Greek Bible (Judg. 11:34) renders the adjectives as *monogenés* (only) and *agapeté* (beloved). Cf. the use of these two adjectives for Jesus: *monogenés* in John 3:16; *agapetós* in Mark 1:11; 9:7.

33. The historical problems posed by Genesis 14 are not pertinent to this literary analysis.

34. Since I use the sacrifice of Isaac as a foil for the story of Jephthah's daughter, I shall not offer here my own literary study of Genesis 22. For a classic interpretation, see Erich Auerbach, "Odysseus' Scar," *Mimesis* (New York: Doubleday & Co., 1957), pp. 1–20; also see George W. Coats, "Abraham's Sacrifice of Faith: A Form-Critical Study of Genesis 22," *Int* 27 (1973): 389–400; James Crenshaw, "Journey into Oblivion: A Structural Analysis of Gen. 22:1–19," *Soundings* 58 (1975): 243–56; Jacob Licht, *Storytelling in the Bible* (Jerusalem: Magnes Press, 1978), pp. 115–20; James Crenshaw, *A Whirlpool of Torment: Israelite Traditions of God as an Oppressive Presence* (Philadelphia: Fortress Press, 1984), pp. 9–29. Comparisons of these two stories stem from ancient times; see, e.g., Robert J. Daly, "The Soteriological Significance of the Sacrifice of Isaac," *CBQ* 39 (1977): 60–62; P. R. Davies and B. D. Chilton, "The Aqedah: A Revised Tradition History," *CBQ* 40 (1978): 521, 526–27; also S. Kierkegaard, *Fear and Trembling* (Princeton, N.J.: Princeton University Press, 1952), pp. 85–87. For a structuralist comparison, see Edmund Leach, "The Legitimacy of Solomon: Some Structural Aspects of Old Testament History," in *Introduction to Structuralism*, ed. Michael Lane (New York: Basic Books, 1970), pp. 256–58. For a comparison based on game theory, see Steven J. Brams, *Biblical Games: A Strategic Analysis of Stories in the Old Testament* (Cambridge, Mass.: MIT Press, 1980), pp. 36–53.

35. Cf. e.g., Gen. 37:29, 34; 44:13; 2 Sam. 13:19, 31; 2 Kings 2:12; Job 1:20; Isa. 36:22, Jer. 41:5.

36. For this rendering of *'āhâ*, see Boling, *Judges*, p. 208.

37. On calamity (*ʿkr*), cf. 1 Sam. 14:29, which is also in the context of an oath to Yahweh; see below, notes 41 and 43.

38. Cf. Jephthah's use of the infinitive absolute here with his similar usage of this grammatical construction in the vow (11:30).

39. This *you* of the daughter is juxtaposed to the *I* (*'ānōkî*) of Jephthah

in the clause that follows: "*You* have become my calamity, for *I* have opened my mouth. . . ." Cf. the use of similar pronouns for emphasis and contrast, also in the words of Jephthah, in 11:7, 9.

40. See Boling, *Judges*, pp. 206, 208–9.

41. To be sure, the circumstances of Absalom's death differ from those of Jephthah's daughter. I note only various responses of fathers to the deaths, actual or potential, of their children. Another instance is Saul's proclaiming a death sentence upon Jonathan, who unknowingly broke his father's oath (*šěbûʿāh*; cf. *neder*, vow) by eating honey (1 Sam. 14:24–46). In that case, the father, like Jephthah, is committed to fulfilling the sentence; the people, however, intercede to save Jonathan. See Keith W. Whitelam, *The Just King*, JSOT Supp. 12 (Sheffield: JSOT Press, 1979), pp. 73–83.

42. Observe that the ominous word burnt offering (*ʿ ôlāh*) occurs only once: in the vow itself, which Jephthah spoke before the identity of the "comer-forth" was known (11:31). After the daughter is specified as the victim, the sacrifice is always alluded to by circumlocution—in the language of Jephthah, his daughter, and the narrator. Truly, the deed is unspeakable.

43. Cf. the similar response of Jonathan to Saul (1 Sam. 14:43). Like this daughter, that son knew that he could not escape the oath of his father despite the earlier flouting of it (1 Sam. 14:29–30). Unlike this daughter, however, Jonathan was a *guilty* victim whose life was spared.

44. For the reading *wander*, see Burney, *Judges*, p. 323; Boling, *Judges*, p. 209.

45. See Lloyd R. Bailey, Sr., *Biblical Perspectives on Death* (Philadelphia: Fortress Press, 1979), pp. 47–51.

46. But cf. Kurt Weitzmann, "The Jephthah Panel in the Bema of the Church of St. Catherine's Monastery on Mount Sinai," *Studies in the Arts at Sinai* (Princeton, N.J.: Princeton University Press, 1982), pp. 341–52. This panel is a counterpart to the Abraham panel; the sacrifices of the daughter and Isaac are prefigurations of Christ's eucharistic sacrifice.

47. Cf. a similar pattern suggested by the references to Mizpah in 10:17 and 11:11; see note 19 above.

48. Cf. the legend of the Cretan king Idomeneus who, after being saved from drowning, vowed to sacrifice to Neptune the first person Idomeneus met on shore. Idamente his son was that person. Before the sacrifice is carried out, Neptune comes to the rescue. On this legend, see Mozart's opera *Idomeneo*. For other Greek parallels, cf. Aeschylus I, *Oresteia*, The Complete Greek Tragedies, ed. David Grene and Richard Lattimore (Chicago: University of Chicago Press, 1957); Euripides IV, *Iphigenia in Aulis*, The Complete Greek Tragedies, ed. David Grene and Richard Lattimore (Chicago: University of Chicago Press, 1958), pp. 210–300. Cf. Yannis Sakellarakis and Efi Sapouna-Sakellarakis, "Drama of Death in a Minoan Temple," *National Geographic* 159 (1981): 205–22.

49. Cf. Ps. 22:1; Matt. 27:46; Mark 15:34.

50. See E. Kautzsch, *Gesenius' Hebrew Grammar* (Oxford: At the Clarendon Press, 1952), § 122q.

51. See F. E. König, *Historisch-comparative Syntax der Herbräischen Sprache: Schulusstheil des Historisch-knitschen Lehregebäudes des Hebräischen* (1897), § 323h; *contra* Burney, *Judges*, pp. 324–25.

52. *Custom* is the translation in the KJV, RSV, JB, NAB, and NJV and also in Boling, *Judges*, p. 207. The NEB, on the other hand, reads *tradition*. In English the two words overlap in meaning. For a parallel usage of the word *ḥōq* (though with a different grammatical construction), see 2 Chron. 35:25, a passage that reports lamentations for the dead king Josiah by male and *female* singers "to this day" (cf. "year by year," Judg. 11:40). Chanting these dirges for the king became a tradition (*ḥōq*) for Israel. Cf. Jacob M. Myers, *II Chronicles*, Anchor Bible (New York: Doubleday & Co., 1965), pp. 214–16.

53. On the problem of the Hebrew infinitive translated here "to mourn," see the commentaries, especially Moore, *Judges*, pp. 303–4. On the basis of Judg. 11:40, some scholars claim that the entire story is aetiological; often they cite parallels in world literature: e.g., Martin Noth, *Aufsätze zur biblischen Landes und Alterumskunde*, I (Neukirchen-Vluyn: Neukirchener Verlag, 1971), pp. 360–65; Theodor H. Gaster, *Myth, Legend, and Custom in the Old Testament* (New York: Harper & Row, 1969), pp. 430–32; Flemming Friis Hvidberg, *Weeping and Laughter in the Old Testament* (Leiden: E. J. Brill, 1962), pp. 103–5; cf. Burney, *Judges*, pp. 332–34; Moore, *Judges*, p. 305. Though illuminating, such approaches tend to neglect the particularity of the story, including its Yahwistic setting. See Boling, *Judges*, pp. 209–10; Green, *The Role of Human Sacrifice in the Ancient Near East*, p. 162.

54. Cf. the living memorial established for Tamar, another daughter of Israel who died childless, though under circumstances different from the daughter of Jephthah (2 Sam. 13:1–20): her brother Absalom named his own daughter Tamar (2 Sam. 14:27). See chapter 2 above. See also Stanley Brice Frost, "The Memorial of the Childless Man," *Int* 26 (1972): 437–50.

55. This conclusion of the Jephthah narrative is structured similarly to other sections with direct discourse surrounding narrated discourse. Note also the use of interrogative sentences.

56. Observe that Jephthah's speech to the Ephraimites (12:2–3) recapitulates in part some of the language of his vow and of the narrator's subsequent summary, but it stops short of any reference to the sacrifice (cf. 11:30–32).

57. Cf. Judg. 10:2, 5; 12:10, 12, 15.

58. Be the noun translated *sons* or *children*, note the irony in reference to Jephthah.

59. In contrast to the scant allusion in the Apocrypha, the pseudepigraphical work *The Book of Biblical Antiquities* (Pseudo-Philo, chapters 39–40) retells the story of Jephthah and his daughter. The point of view differs strikingly from that in the canonical literature. God criticizes Jephthah harshly for his wicked vow; his daughter, given the name Seila, dies willingly so that her sacrificial death would not be in vain; and God decrees that she is wiser than both her father and "the wise men of the people." See Daniel J. Harrington, Jacques Cazeaux, Charles Perrot, and Pierre-Maurice Bogaert, *Pseudo-Philon: Les Antiquities Bibliques, Sources Chrétiennes* 229–30 (Paris: LeCerf, 1976), vol. I, pp. 273–85; vol. II, pp. 186–93. Jewish legend holds that in death Jephthah was punished by dismemberment. See Louis Ginzberg, *The Legends of the Jews*, IV (Philadelphia:

Jewish Publication Society of America, 1968), pp. 43–47. In the twelfth century, the view was put forward that the daughter was not sacrificed but rather subjected to solitary confinement; see Moore, *Judges*, p. 304. But seclusion is living death; cf. the plight of Tamar in chapter 2 above. Whether secluded or sacrificed, the female is the innocent victim of violence.

60. Cf. the responses of readers throughout the centuries in literature, art, music; see Wilbur Owen Sypherd, *Jephthah and his Daughter* (Newark: University of Delaware, 1948); also *Encyclopaedia Judaica* 9 (Jerusalem: Keter Publishing House, 1978), cols. 1343–45. For a psychoanalytic interpretation, see Robert Seidenberg, "Sacrificing the First You See," *The Psychoanalytic Review* 53 (1966): 49–62.

in memoriam

THE DAUGHTER OF JEPHTHAH

AN UNNAMED WOMAN

TAMAR

HAGAR

Indexes

AUTHORS AND EDITORS

HEBREW WORDS

SCRIPTURE

OLD TESTAMENT

NEW TESTAMENT

SUBJECTS

Abraham/Abram, 9, 10, 11, 12, 13, 16, 18–19, 20, 21–22, 23, 26, 27, 28, 29n. 3, 31n. 14, 33n. 40, 34 nn. 53, 57; 35n. 71, 80, 88n. 18, 101, 102, 105
Absalom, 38, 39, 40–41, 46, 49–52, 53, 54, 55, 58n. 5, 62 nn. 56, 60, 64; 63 nn. 66, 67, 70, 72; 84, 114n. 41, 115n. 54
Achsah, 90n. 52
Affliction, 13–14, 16, 17, 32 nn. 32, 35
Ammon/Ammonites, 37, 84, 93–94, 95, 96, 97, 98, 99, 110n. 12, 111n. 19
Amnon, 38–50, 51–52, 53, 54, 55, 56, 58 nn. 18, 28, 31; 60 nn. 31, 35; 62 nn. 56, 60, 62; 63 nn. 66, 72; 84, 89n. 41
Angel of the Lord, 35n. 71, 80, 105. *See also* Divine messengers
Annunciations, 16–18, 19, 28, 32n. 30, 33n. 41
Apocrypha, 107–8

Baal Hazor, 55
Barrenness, 9, 10–11, 12, 31n. 16, 84, 104, 106
Bathsheba, 37, 62n. 62, 84
Beersheba, 23, 24, 82
Benjamin/Benjaminites, 65, 71, 76, 79, 82–83, 84, 85, 87n. 5
Benjaminite traditions, 65, 82, 85
Bethlehem, 65, 66, 67, 68, 70, 71, 73, 80, 85, 88n. 28
Bible, 2, 3, 6n. 10, 18
Births, 9, 18–20. *See also* Annunciations
Blessing, 4–5
Boaz, 85
Burnt offering, 96, 101, 102, 114n. 42

Caleb, 90n. 52
Canaan, 9, 13, 20
Chiasmus, 43, 46, 47, 48, 58n. 13, 60n. 42, 61 nn. 46, 47, 50
Child/children, 9, 10, 12, 13, 16–17, 18–19, 24, 25–27, 38, 53–54, 102, 104, 114n. 41. *See also* Daughter(s); Sons
Christ, 114n. 46

Christ figures, 3
Church, early, 3, 87
Circular structures, 10, 11, 37, 38, 39, 50, 51, 53, 60 nn. 33, 40; 62 nn. 59, 64; 65. *See also* Inclusio; Ring composition
Classism, x, 28, 29, 35n. 76
Clothes, rending of, 50, 101
Concubines, 11, 30n. 13, 66. *See also* Unnamed woman

Dan, 82
Daughter of Jephthah, 1, 88n. 25, 93–109, 115n. 59
Daughter of old man in Gibeah, 66, 74, 75, 76
Daughters of Lot, 75
Daughters of Shiloh, 83
David, 37–38, 39, 41, 42, 43, 45–46, 49, 50, 52, 53–54, 55, 58n. 14, 59 nn. 18, 20, 31; 62 nn. 56, 60, 62; 63 nn. 70, 72; 84, 100, 102, 108
Death, 24–25, 98–101, 104, 105–6, 114n. 41. *See also* Murder; Sacrifice
Descendants, 16, 22, 26, 27, 28, 32n. 27, 104
Desire, 40, 47, 58n. 6, 60n. 41, 62n. 66
Desolation, 9–29, 48, 50, 52
Deuteronomic editor, 65, 93
Dinah, 67
Dismemberment, 2, 80–81, 82, 83, 115n. 93
Divine messengers, 4, 7n. 17, 14–18, 19, 25–26, 28, 31n. 23, 80, 105
Divine promise, 9, 16–17, 19, 22, 26, 28
Divorce, 34n. 57

Egypt, 13, 14, 21, 27, 30n. 8, 35n. 74
Egyptian women, 31n. 16
Elders of Gilead, 94–95, 96, 110n. 8, 111 nn. 14, 16, 17, 18, 19; 112n. 20
Eli, 84
Elimelech, 85
Elisha, 32n. 30
Elizabeth, 32n. 30
Elkanah, 84
End-stress, 55, 62n. 64
Ephraim/Ephraimites, 65, 66, 70, 79–80, 84, 107, 115n. 56